'I highly recommend L … *es,*
where the reader is po … *nd*
faithful work of God … ts
and Open Roads *ser* … *is*
impossible for the great God we serve, whether we find ourselves up against spiritual opposition, lack of resources, tight deadlines, or even huge personal loss. God is still on the throne and His power is at work across the globe through His people. Read it and be encouraged!'

Liz Parker, missionary with Mission Aviation Fellowship and author of *Immeasurably More*

'What a page turner! David Robinson's account of his years as a missionary makes exciting and inspiring reading. Definitely a missionary autobiography not to be missed.'

Tony Lane, Professor of Historical Theology at the London School of Theology

'A fascinating insight into a missionary's life and how God worked through him.'

John Butterworth, award-winning journalist, editor and author of *God's Secret Listener* and *God's Needle*

'In our world of competing choices, this book could be challengingly subtitled "This one thing I do" (Phil 3:13). David's life as a church planter in rural Thailand, and Team Leader in Cambodia exemplifies this singular commitment to obey God. Through sufferings and loss, joys and triumphs the book illustrates powerfully the Lord's faithfulness and

sovereignty in all circumstances. This is authentic David, as I have known him, through his 50 years in mission, pursuing his goal: "one thing I do" in following Christ. Read the book and follow David's example.'

David Pickard, former General Director of OMF International

MUD BULLETS AND OPEN ROADS

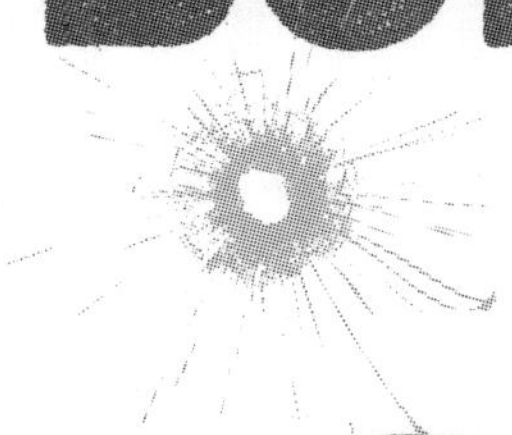

DAVID ROBINSON

10 Publishing
a division of 10 of those.com

First published in Great Britain in 2024

British Library Cataloguing in Publication Data
A record for this book is available from the British Library

ISBN: 978-1-837280-28-5

Designed by Pete Barnsley (CreativeHoot.com)

Printed in Denmark

10Publishing, a division of 10ofthose.com
Unit C, Tomlinson Road, Leyland, PR25 2DY, England

Email: info@10ofthose.com
Website: www.10ofthose.com

1 3 5 7 10 8 6 4 2

CONTENTS

PART TWO – BULLETS: CAMBODIA

PART THREE – OPEN ROADS: THE UK

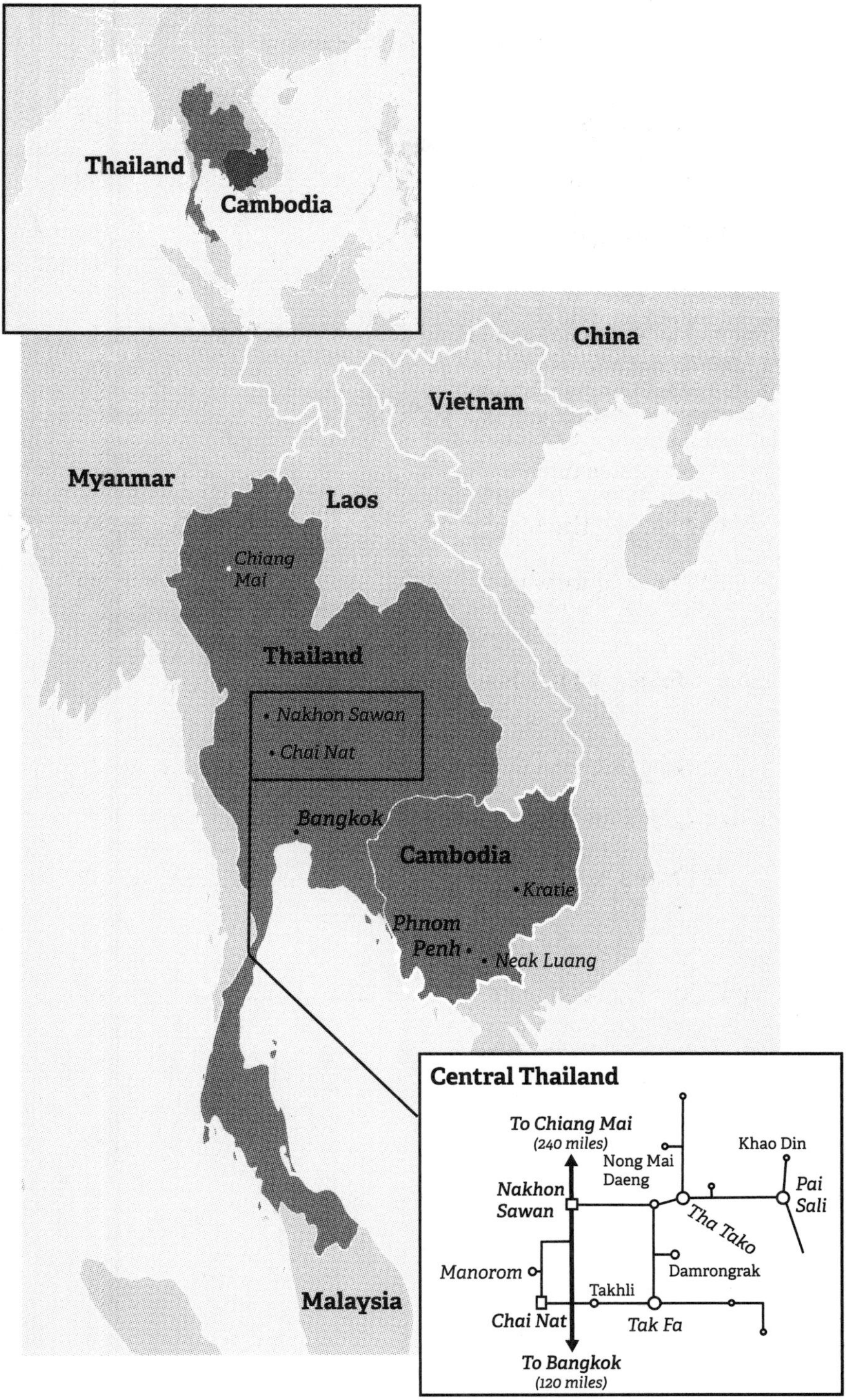
Thailand
Cambodia
China
Vietnam
Myanmar
Laos
Chiang Mai
Thailand
Nakhon Sawan
Chai Nat
Bangkok
Cambodia
Kratie
Phnom Penh
Neak Luang
Malaysia
Central Thailand
To Chiang Mai
(240 miles)
Khao Din
Nong Mai Daeng
Nakhon Sawan
Pai Sali
Tha Tako
Manorom
Damrongrak
Takhli
Chai Nat
Tak Fa
To Bangkok
(120 miles)

PROLOGUE

It's not every day you foil an assassination plot.

On Sunday 8 August 1982, I was bouncing along the dirt road in the local bus – a converted truck – while sweating in 40-degree heat. I got chatting about spiritual things to the small, wiry man sitting next to me. After a while, he told me about a dream in which he had leprosy but had been cured through a Western man who looked a little like me.

'What do you think of the dream?' he asked.

'Could it be you're about to experience something special?' I ventured.

I learned his name was Mr Gram and he lived in a nearby village. Clearly he didn't have leprosy, so I wondered if God was preparing him for something deeper than physical healing.

As we journeyed on, I told him I was here to share the good news that God had provided new life for those who trust in Jesus, his Son. He was keen to learn more despite the loud engine noise and swirling dust. So before I got off the bus, I promised to visit him in his village and share more of the good news.

A few weeks later I visited Gram and received a warm welcome. Over the next few weeks I shared the gospel message with him and his family, and was delighted when he and some family members prayed to accept Jesus as their Lord and Saviour.

I was curious to know more about Mr Gram's life and work. 'I assemble a group of workmen, and we go and build houses,' he told me. 'But,' he continued, 'I also have another job: I'm an assassin! On the day you met me on the bus, I was going on a job to kill someone! After meeting you, though, I changed my mind. Something must have spoken inside me. So I got off the bus, crossed the road, and took the next bus home.'

I was astonished at how the Lord had used my presence on the bus that day to prevent a murder and change the direction of Mr Gram's life. I was reminded that we who are led by the Lord truly are the 'fragrance' of life or death to those we meet day by day (2 Corinthians 2:15, NLT).

Having given up his sideline in assassinations, Mr Gram became a key figure in the small Christian group that began meeting in his village. Later, when the Christians in the nearby town of Tha Tako wanted to construct a church building, they naturally turned to Mr Gram to arrange the work. What fruit from a chance meeting on a bus and what a difference from my work as an electrical engineer in Manchester!

PART ONE

MUD

THAILAND

1

THREE CROWDS

'This is mass hysteria,' I thought. 'I am not going to go forward!' I was sitting in the stands of Manchester City football ground, watching a stream of people responding to American evangelist Billy Graham's appeal to come to Christ.

The picture he painted of the exalted Christ returning in glory massively impacted me. Billy Graham preached from Mark 8:38, which says that on the day when the Lord Jesus returns, he will be ashamed of those who are ashamed of him now. I realised that included me. But I did not go forward. I needed to know first what this all meant.

At the time I was an apprentice at Associated Electrical Industries. I had gone to hear Billy Graham because my supervisor, Fred, who was a committed Christian, had urged me to go. Even though I had grown up going to church, I didn't have much of a faith of my own. So the next day I was full of questions.

'What am I missing?' I asked Fred. 'What does it mean to become a real Christian?' We began to talk, and walked the length and breadth of the factory until all my questions were answered!

The following day I returned to the stadium, where Billy Graham was speaking once again. This time, when the invitation came to make a commitment to Christ, I walked forward to receive him as my Lord and Saviour. The date is written in my Bible: 17 June 1961. I was 18 years old.

I walked out of the stadium knowing I had become a new person, now with my own relationship with God. Immediately I began telling my friends and family about how I had met Jesus and what he had done for me. My family didn't appreciate being preached to but recognised a big change in my life. However, I still understood very little about my newfound faith.

Surprisingly, it was in the next stage of my apprenticeship with Associated Electrical Industries that God provided the help I needed to grow in my faith. In September 1961 I began a degree course in engineering at Bristol University. Here members of the Christian Union spotted this very 'worldly' new Christian and helped me begin to put my faith into practice.

One of the first lessons I learned was the importance of obeying the Lord in my personal life. I loved ballroom dancing and took strong objection to the fact that the main meetings of the Christian Union were held on

Saturday evenings, clashing with the weekly dances at the Students' Union. 'If you want to grow as a Christian,' my new Christian friends told me, 'you need to come and hear our regular Bible teaching.'

For several months I 'held out'. I enjoyed the excitement of the dances. Then one night, after buying tickets for the Saturday dance, I felt God prompting me about whether there was something better for me. So I ripped up the tickets and went to the CU meeting instead. From then on I committed myself to the Christian group and my faith began to grow. After three years of weekly Bible expositions from gifted teachers and the influence of godly friends, I was given a good foundation in the Christian faith. From my attitude to the opposite sex to prayer and reading the Bible and even to cleaning up my speech, my whole life was being changed. Over 60 years later I am still in touch with godly mentors from those days in Bristol and still have some of the Christian books they gave me.

With university behind me, I was settling down to the happy prospect of a career in engineering, beginning with five years working with my firm as 'pay back' for the apprenticeship and university tuition. But a new shock awaited me. At the final meeting of the 1965 Keswick Convention, three thousand of us were gathered in the big tent to hear the missionaries' stories of the amazing things they had seen on the other side of the world. 'Why are they speaking with such earnestness?' I wondered.

I guessed that they would challenge us to become missionaries too. 'Happily that doesn't apply to me,' I thought. 'I can't become a missionary. I still have five more years on my contract.'

But then an inner voice said, 'That's not your problem; that's my problem.'

Somewhat surprised, I continued to reason, 'But I don't have the ability to be a missionary. I haven't led anyone to Christ.' The inner voice gave me the same answer as before.

'What about the danger and the struggles of language learning? I only just scraped my French exams.' Same answer!

All my objections were dealt with in the same way. It was much like how the Lord had answered Moses' objections in Exodus 3, when the Lord met him in the burning bush. Perhaps God was calling me to be a missionary?

As I had guessed, the meeting closed with a challenge for people to stand up if they would commit their lives to God for full-time Christian service.

I stood.

Once again my life had been redirected. I walked out of the tent dazed by the decision I had just made, and with little idea where I would be heading.

2

A NEW DIRECTION

My commitment at Keswick had been to 'whole-time service at home or abroad'. It must be for overseas missionary work, I reasoned, as I had already done extensive travel overseas, including an overland journey to India. However, I realised that I knew little of what missionaries did, or whether I was fit for the task. The objections I had raised at the Keswick meeting were all still valid!

I now had a window of opportunity to work on these objections. With my five-year engineering apprenticeship behind me, I was required to work for the firm for a further five years. And so, while working in Manchester, I could also work through the challenges in turn. Though I had a grounding in the faith from my time at university, I didn't have anyone to guide me in the way ahead, but as an engineer I felt a systematic approach was needed!

First, if I was going to be a missionary, I needed to find out what that really meant. So each year I went to the annual conference of a missionary society serving in a different continent. In turn I ticked off East Asia, Europe, South America, and India. At each conference I assessed whether these were people I could serve with, looking at their aims and methods, and discovering how successful they were!

Next, I realised I needed to increase my Bible knowledge. So I enrolled in a Bible correspondence course with a university theology department. This was not very successful, as without guidance in choosing the course, I found I was studying material that did not accept the Bible as the authoritative word of God. Nevertheless, understanding wider Bible scholarship would in fact be valuable in the future.

One of my main objections at Keswick was my lack of ministry experience. In this area I was much more successful. I felt it important to be part of a local church, so joined a small Independent Methodist church in Stretford, Manchester. Here I was able to get involved in all aspects of hands-on church life. I organised a small team to do door-to-door evangelism on Saturday mornings, with some open-air meetings. I grew in confidence in sharing the gospel, though I still didn't have a chance to lead anyone to Christ – another of my objections at Keswick.

So to develop my evangelistic skills, for two summers I joined outreach weeks in the UK. These were organised by Operation Mobilisation, a newly formed agency which helped young people gain experience in serving the Lord through its focus on evangelism and gospel book sales. Here finally I had the joy of leading two or three people to Christ.

Soon, however, I would face a whole new set of unexpected questions that would test my commitment at Keswick.

The Catacombs was a Christian cellar café in the centre of Manchester. With subdued lighting and wall paintings on the brick walls, it had live music from Christian rock bands, free coffee, and friendly chat. The aim was to share the gospel with young people, especially those hanging out on the streets of the city. Teams of helpers came from local churches, and learned how to share their faith with those invited in. I could be found there most Saturday nights for two years, either handing out invitation leaflets in the surrounding streets, or talking at length with those who came in.

One Saturday in 1968, I was brushing the floor at the bottom of the stairs, ready for opening, when two young ladies arrived, expecting to join the team. I stopped brushing and took time to welcome them. One I vaguely recognised as Rhona, but didn't know her companion.

Rhona introduced me to her friend Jenny, who was coming to the Catacombs for the first time. When Jenny introduced herself, she had a beautiful melodic voice – I discovered later she was a speech therapist.

I was pleased when Jenny joined the outreach team as there seemed to be some mutual attraction, but we were serving on different days of the week. Occasionally there were joint team days, so I made a point of getting to know her then. Jenny was fairly tall and slim with long dark hair and an infectious warm smile. I also observed a maturity I had not found in other girls. In early 1969 I invited her to join our local church outreach team in Stretford. As our friendship blossomed, I remembered that a friend, after meeting Jenny, had told me, 'You should marry that girl!' Should I follow the advice?

I wondered how to find out if she shared my sense of God's calling to overseas mission. If she didn't, I knew our relationship couldn't proceed as I was still intent on following God's direction for my life. Shortly afterwards we attended a weekend conference for a missionary society serving Central Asia, and I got the answer. At the end of the event, the speaker challenged people to offer their lives for missionary service, as and when God called them. I did not know how Jenny had responded, but on the way back I asked her. I was thrilled to hear that she had committed herself to serve cross-culturally.

So in May 1969 I proposed to Jenny on one of our Saturday morning outreaches! She graciously accepted, we completed the outreach, and then went into Altrincham to buy an engagement ring! It was a promising start to a life of service together.

Of course, this brought many more questions: When should we get married? Where should we live? When should we head overseas? And where did God want us to serve him?

We realised that if we bought a house and settled down, we would probably never enter into overseas mission. So we agreed to leave our jobs at the end of August, marry mid-September, and go directly to Bible college 10 days later!

At London Bible College we learned not only about the biblical foundations of our faith, pastoral care, and preaching, but also a practical lesson in how to lean on the Lord for provision. Our savings would only cover the first year of the course. We found that as we prayed, though, God provided for our second year through a government grant and made up the rest through generous gifts from friends!

As our thoughts turned to where we would serve, we went to the annual conference of OMF, a missionary society serving in East Asia. The OMF conference had been first on my list of mission events to attend five years earlier. To my surprise, we met an elderly lady who not only remembered me from last time, but told me she had been praying ever since that God would guide me for the way ahead! This level of dependence on the Lord impacted me, and helped assure us this was an organisation with which we would be happy to serve.

We learned that OMF had been serving in East Asia for over 100 years, first in China, then in other East Asian countries. It was a 'faith mission' relying on God alone for the supply of funds in answer to prayer. Their work emphasised evangelism and church planting, something that resonated with our hearts. At Bible college we had done outreach among Chinese people, and connected well with them. So we put in our application forms, and were accepted. Truly, God's promise that 'I will instruct you and teach you in the way you should go' (Psalm 32:8) was happening with us!

This continued even as we had to delay our departure for a year following the birth of our first baby, Hannah. That year gave us time to adjust to life as family and to visit churches we hoped would pray for and support us. I also found work in the office of the Manchester City Mission, a valuable preparation for my future work in mission administration and leadership.

It was then time to pack our stuff to send on ahead. All we would need for four years (including three mosquito nets and lots of toys) had to be squashed into five insect-resistant boxes! Finally, at a special meeting at church, we were prayed over with the laying on of hands. Now we were ready for take-off!

3

A NEW LAND

The morning of 20 September 1972 dawned cold and dull in Manchester. However, the weather failed to dampen our excitement or that of the friends and family who came to the main train station to say goodbye. Our first stopover was at the OMF centre at Newington Green in London, joining other new missionaries flying out to the headquarters in Singapore for the six-week orientation course. Well-wishers there gave us each a Bible verse – mine was 'Do not be afraid ... the Lord your God goes with you; he will never leave you' (Deuteronomy 31:6). Stepping forward into the unknown was to be our constant experience. Fears I experienced could have kept me from following the Lord's pathway, but this solid promise of his presence was to be my constant mainstay in the days ahead.

Arriving in Singapore, we met our first challenge – the sweltering heat! We drove up a long, palm tree-lined drive to the OMF headquarters, a large Chinese villa with curved roofs. That was to be our home for the next six weeks of the orientation course. Soon we were mingling with other missionary recruits arriving from Europe and North America – wondering how we would all get along together! We clicked with a Canadian couple, Koos and Colleen Fietje, and their baby son, Michael. Hannah had early 'bonding' with Michael as they shared a double pram on walks to the nearby Botanic Gardens.

We quickly learned how to sleep under mosquito nets, keep up our fluid intake, and walk down the street without sweating too much. Our main task was learning the skills we would need to master an oriental language. The rest of the time was filled with new experiences: bargaining in Chinese bazaars, exploring old colonial districts, and practising using chopsticks.

Having given OMF an open offer that we would be willing to serve anywhere, we also found out at the orientation course where we would be placed for the next four years: Thailand. We were excited about the opportunities for evangelism there, and delighted to find that our friends, the Fietjes, would be joining us. While Jenny, Colleen, and the two children would fly to Bangkok, Koos and I – with two other new workers – went by train in order to ensure all our heavy boxes were transported safely.

This three-day journey northwards – from Singapore, through west Malaysia, and then to southern Thailand – was an eye-opening experience. Miles and miles of rubber plantations and green rice paddy fields stretched out before us on either side of the train. Men and women with wide straw hats tended crops, dredged water channels, fished in between the rice plants, or steered one of their little craft up the water channels. Brightly coloured Buddhist temples standing among the trees; each had their cluster of wooden homes for the saffron-robed monks gathered around them.

When we arrived in Bangkok, where we would be based for language study in our first year, the scene shifted to the noise, dirt, and bustle of an overcrowded city. One of the first things I noticed was that all the homes had what looked like colourful 'bird tables' in the gardens, but there didn't seem to be many birds. We soon discovered these were shrines for the local spirits, thought to guard each property. We knew we would have to learn the language, but now realised how much we had to learn about Thai culture as well.

Within days we were sent 150 miles northwards by train to Nakhon Sawan, where we would celebrate our first Christmas in Asia. This was the principal town of a large province of the same name where many of our missionaries were working. Some of these missionaries met us and took us to their home by bicycle pedicabs, a new and somewhat scary experience! Here our daughter, Hannah, marked her first birthday by taking her first few steps, while we got to grips with squat toilets, malaria and dysentery pills, and boiling our drinking water.

Back in Bangkok, keeping healthy was an ongoing challenge. A real test was when Hannah got severe dysentery and had to be carefully nursed for several nerve-wracking days. Not being used to the severity of tropical diseases, we prayed earnestly for the Lord to help us. We were now learning to take hold of the Lord's promise 'I am with you always' (Matthew 28:20) as once again we looked to him in faith in a testing situation. The answer came through one of our new workers, a qualified doctor, who took over Hannah's care and gently nursed her back to health and safety. We thanked God knowing we could move forward in peace and confidence in his care.

Most of our first year in Bangkok was spent in language school and being introduced to the mysteries of the Thai language. I found learning it incredibly difficult because Thai has many unusual features for an English speaker. It is a tonal language, meaning that changing the tone of a word changes its meaning. For example, the word 'maa' can mean a 'horse' or a 'dog', depending on its tone! In addition, not only are Thai letters written with strange characters, but there are no gaps between the words!

So that first year, our progress in learning Thai was painfully slow, made slower still by the fact Jenny and I had to take turns caring for Hannah while the other studied. Speaking practice was difficult too, as many Bangkok residents had a fair amount of English that they wanted to use on us, rather than the other way round! Trying to speak Thai was always a scary experience, but the Lord was with us even in our frequent miscommunications!

We were beginning to gain the skills we needed to live in a rural situation where we would be immersed in Thai language and culture.

Our first year was also an opportunity to explore what future ministry might look like. A four-week visit to central Thailand – the rice-growing plain to the north of Bangkok – opened our eyes to the deep spiritual needs there, with very few Christians. The people were friendly and welcomed the opportunity to talk with us. Nevertheless, almost no one spoke English, underlining the need to persevere with our language learning.

After this visit, we felt sure that was a place we would be happy to serve. We had heard that spiritually it would be hard ground, but were assured that where God led he would provide. And so it was agreed that after completing our year in Bangkok, we would move to central Thailand for the next three years. We were excited to see what the Lord now had in store for us.

4

FORWARD IN WEAKNESS

Towards the end of 1973, we moved 150 miles north of Bangkok to the county town of Chai Nat, where we were now to be based. We were in central Thailand, an area that had historically seen little response to the gospel. After 30 years of persevering work by a large OMF team, less than 1000 had believed. But was God about to work powerfully here? Even with our limited language, would we be able to make an effective contribution?

Our first step was to settle into a large, old wooden house which had been rented for us on the main street. Being on stilts, it was nice and cool, as fresh air came up through the floorboards. We inherited a gaggle of geese who roamed in the garden and became quite possessive of us at times. When visitors talked too long or too loudly, the geese would locate themselves under the floor and honk to signal it was time for them to leave!

We soon realised that, with the heat and dust, the necessary daily chores of washing clothes, mopping floors and shopping for food in the fresh market, we would have little time for ministry. So, like most missionary homes at the time, we decided to employ a house-helper. Now with Mrs Noi to help us (not just in housekeeping but in language practice!) we had time to do regular language study and also had opportunities to get involved in ministry. Where should I focus?

I especially wanted to try some outreach ministry, and one of the first opportunities to do so came in March 1974. The rice fields were hard, brown soil, and the farmers had nothing much to do. So, seizing this opportunity, a team of missionaries and local Christians from the area were travelling by Land Rover to a number of villages that had no church. Once there, they shared the gospel using films and testimonies. I was keen to join them and see what happened.

We first toured the village, giving an invitation by loudspeaker to an evening film show. People were excited by the prospect of free entertainment on their doorstep. We erected a large screen in a nearby field, and as it grew dark, the crowds began to gather to watch the programme of films. Up to 200 people sat for hours watching the gospel films, projected from the back of the Land Rover. While the reels were being changed, they heard testimonies from Thai Christians. Food sellers made the most of this community gathering, while I was often found selling gospel booklets. The next day we visited homes around the village to explain the gospel message further. We did not often see much response, but we trusted this gospel 'seed sowing' would bear fruit in the future.

Despite having little Thai language, I inherited from a retired missionary a Bible class in the Chai Nat town prison. Every two weeks I would be taken from the huge entry gate to a small study room overlooking the prisoners' exercise yard. The half-dozen class members would be brought in by a guard, and we would all be locked in. Its members had committed robbery, assault, and murder – not perhaps the choicest of companions! 'With my limited Thai language, it's fine if you don't want me to come,' I offered, but they insisted I should keep coming. As we persevered with a simple Bible study course, my Thai language gradually improved. Over the next two and a half years, trust and friendship grew too. Remarkably, during that time most of them accepted Christ as their Saviour! The Lord was dispelling my earliest doubts that I could be fruitful in his service.

I also wanted to find ways to share the gospel with people in the town. Having discovered that there was a market up by the river every week, one day I loaded a table, chair, awning, and a stack of books on to a little trolley cart I had made. Then, with much trepidation, I set off for the market. People seemed somewhat taken aback by this tall foreigner invading their territory, but eventually found me a place to set up.

I don't think I sold many books, but I had lots of good chats with people who stopped by, and who seemed to get a kick out of talking to me. Some began to open their minds to the wonder of the gospel, and to take the first steps of faith.

While I had growing ministry opportunities in evangelism and in helping local churches, for Jenny ministry was less straightforward. For a while she taught English at a local school, but her primary role was to care for our toddler, Hannah, and to run the home. This meant she had less time for language learning, and her limited Thai language made relating to neighbours difficult. Like many missionary mums, she found herself restricted to the home, and loneliness was a real issue at times. For both of us, learning to trust the Lord for protection and care was essential.

Towards the end of 1974 our first year in Chai Nat, Jenny was pregnant again and had several months of severe morning sickness. Then in December I got hepatitis. So we both had to move over to Manorom, about seven miles away, to be cared for at the OMF hospital. We were frustrated with this apparent block to our progress in ministry. Combined with the difficulties of learning the language, adapting to Thai culture, and occasional bouts of homesickness, it sometimes felt like a burden too hard to bear.

Well-meaning advice from people at home suggested that maybe we needed some time back in the UK. Even

Koos, located in another town, commented one day that if an aeroplane stopped at his front gate, he would get on it and go home. I replied that even though things were painful at times, I wouldn't get on it – not because we were superheroes, but because God's call had brought us here, so this is where we would stay until he moved us on. We were assured that he still had lots of work for us to do here. 'My only aim is to finish the race and complete the task the Lord Jesus has given me' (Acts 20:24) was a verse that strengthened my resolve then and on many future occasions.

In January 1975 our second child, Paul, was born. Now Jenny had two young children to look after.

As my health improved and I began regaining my strength, I looked for ministry opportunities beyond Chai Nat. I discovered from my colleagues that there were small pockets of believers in some of the villages in the wider area, the fruit of earlier missionary activity. Maybe I could encourage them by an occasional visit? The problem was that I had no transport. Most people used motorbikes, and clearly that was what I needed. But OMF's provision only covered living expenses. So Jenny and I began to pray. The Lord had reassured us, 'You did not choose me, but I chose you ... so that you might go and bear fruit ... whatever you ask in my name the Father will give you' (John 15:16). We were encouraged to ask even for a motorbike.

One day we noticed that our support level had gone up by £200.

We then discovered a missionary going on home leave was selling his motorbike. The price? £200! We bought the bike, and it served us well for the next few years. After the purchase, our support level went back to its previous level. We were learning to trust God more and more to provide the things that we needed.

My new motorbike enabled me to visit a number of outlying villages to meet Thai Christians, encourage them with God's word, and worship together. I was encouraged by how much the believers appreciated these care visits and by how my ability at speaking Thai was gradually improving with their help and corrections. Riding the roads was not always straightforward, and motorbike accidents were fairly common in the area. Returning from one of these visits, I met a flock of sheep sweeping across the road. Collision was inevitable, leaving me flying along with my upturned bike in one direction, and the sheep fleeing in another! Happily, I only suffered minor injuries – the greater pain was the looks of merriment on the faces of bystanders at seeing this foreigner make a fool of himself.

Recognising that I would be more effective working with a Thai colleague, I was excited when God provided Mr Tawee, a member of a local church about 10 miles from Chai Nat, who was happy to work with me. He was a farmer recovering from leprosy, and was keen to do gospel outreach in his area. So we agreed to give one day a week to visiting local villages, sharing the message with those we met. For me this was also a great language-learning experience, as the words had to be shouted slowly over the motorbike engine!

During our visits, we found one or two lone Christians – there was no church in the area – so we organised some regular small group meetings for them. They in turn reached out to their friends, and several come to Christ. With the converts baptised, a few small meetings started. Was God giving me the 'gift' of being able to gather his people, something never dreamed of in my decision time at Keswick?

Around this time an unexpected incident opened a surprising new line of ministry. Before I went to Thailand, I assumed that other missionaries were always godly, caring, and wonderful people. But I was to discover this wasn't always the case. On one occasion we were on the receiving end of an unjust 'mouthful' from a senior missionary. I was so upset that I could hardly sleep for several nights. Jenny and I recognised this was a strategy of the evil one to divide the Lord's servants and hinder their work. We decided to take action to try and restore the relationship – with marmalade! As this was not available in local shops and was a precious commodity for Western missionaries, we selected our best pot. We then briefly visited the senior missionary, telling her, 'We thought you would like something special,' before leaving.

Wonderfully, God was at work in the situation. The next day the senior missionary called round and apologised for what they had said. It then began to dawn on us that we were there to minister not just to the Thai people we had come to serve, but to our co-workers as well. So we committed to pray for our colleagues and Thai friends. We were encouraged by Paul's words: 'let us do good to all people, especially to those who belong to the family of believers' (Galatians 6:10). This experience taught us the importance of the costly role of restoring good relationships between colleagues. It was a role I would often have to fulfil in the future.

Four years had now passed since we had arrived in Thailand, and it was now time to return to the UK for a period of home leave. The joys and pains of life in Thailand, language learning, ministry attempts, sickness, and accidents had all worked changes in us. Above all, we had learned that we must trust the Lord in every situation.

5

AN OPEN DOOR

It was a strange experience returning 'home' to the UK. While occasional letters, airmail copies of the *Guardian Weekly*, and even a visit from my mother had kept us connected with home, our friends had now visibly aged, familiar shops had disappeared, and new words had entered the language. Hannah and Paul were somewhat overwhelmed being hugged by relatives they had never met before, but seemed to cope well.

Our welcome-home meeting on 2 October 1976 at the Stretford Independent Methodist Church was doubly special. While in Chai Nat, I had found time to do the Independent Methodist minister's training course by correspondence. So our welcome was combined with my induction as a minister of the denomination.

The year in the UK flew by. It was a privilege, at over 130 meetings, to share what God was doing among the small groups of believers we had left behind in Chai Nat. We were so encouraged as we met the many people who had faithfully prayed for and supported us, showing their love for us and for God's kingdom.

Two months before we were due to go back to Thailand, a proposal arrived from the OMF leadership team. Would we be willing to form a team with Koos and Colleen Fietje, and to head to a different area to do church-planting work?

Initially we were very positive. Koos and Colleen had been part of our new worker course in Singapore, and we had enjoyed their friendship in Thailand. Koos, who was gifted in personal evangelism, would be a key part of the team. Colleen, also with young children, would be a good friend to Jenny with similar childcare responsibilities.

However, the more we heard about Tha Tako, the town where we would be based, the more warning bells began to ring. We discovered that this was a place people avoided. Tha Tako district was reputed to have one of the highest murder rates in Thailand.

At the same time Tha Tako was clearly a place with great spiritual need. Although some evangelism had been done there 20 years before, there was nothing now to show for it. There was no church, and no known Christians in the town or in its surrounding district.

Weighing up the situation, we sensed this invitation was from the Lord. In our Bible study times, the verse 'I have placed before you an open door' (Revelation 3:8) came to our attention, and affirmed the Lord's direction and care for us. So with some trepidation we agreed to go.

In September 1977 we began our move there, putting our concerns in the Lord's hands.

An initial visit to Tha Tako, however, revealed that there were no houses for rent. Was this really an open door? Happily, the OMF-run hospital at Manorom, about two hours away, had a guest room where we could 'camp out' and consider our next move. During this waiting period, we were able to take our daughter, Hannah, now five, to the OMF boarding school in north Malaysia, where we could get her settled for the four-month term. Though leaving her there was very hard, it helped knowing she was established with a set of friends.

Visits to Tha Tako continued over several weeks as we still wondered whether God really wanted us there. At least we were able to make friends with one or two people who said they would look out for a place to stay for us.

Eventually Koos and Colleen found a house in the marketplace. Shortly afterwards we located a small, run-down wooden house on stilts on the edge of the rice fields that we felt would be okay for us. It had no glass in the windows, but that kept us cool, and we fitted mesh screening to keep out the mosquitoes and window bars to keep out the robbers.

Occasionally water from the nearby rice fields would overflow into our compound, sometimes up to two feet deep. That was no problem for our neighbours – they all had small boats for doing market shopping, and of course they were happy to take Jenny along too.

By Christmas 1977 we were ready to see how God might use us to bring the gospel to the people of the area. Our first challenge was working out where to begin. We were tasked with reaching not only Tha Tako district, but also the districts of Pai Sali to the east and Tak Fa to the south, both a 40-minute motorbike ride from Tha Tako. I thought I would start by picking up the work I had done before near Tak Fa with Mr Tawee, but for now that door seemed to be closed. He was busy and there were few believers remaining. So I concluded that I should focus on Tha Tako instead and work closely with Koos.

Koos and I knew that the response to the gospel in central Thailand had been very slow in the past. Many of our colleagues saw perhaps one conversion a year. Eager to see something greater than this, we felt more momentum was needed and agreed on three principles. First, we would do intensive outreach the first year, seeking to make some inroads for the gospel in the area. Second, we would commit to working together closely in our evangelism. Third, and most importantly, we would pray for God to guide us to the people he had prepared to come to faith.

As I now joined Koos on his evangelistic walks around town or conversations in cafés, we expected to see God work. Before long there were a handful of people open to hearing more about the Christian faith. Mr Giang, who worked in the local bank, was one of them. He was initially opposed to the gospel, linking it with the Western colonial activity he detested. As we persisted in sharing the good news with him, though, he gradually became more open.

Mr Giang was not alone in his gospel interest. So in February 1978, when one of our new friends asked if we could start a Christian meeting, we agreed. It was to be low-key, comprising a gospel slide show and a meal at Koos' house in the marketplace. To our surprise 18 people showed up, and six of this group decided they wanted to become Christians! Wanting to conserve this 'fruit', we began a weekly 'nurture' meeting for them. Truly God was with us.

Having prayed with these six as they accepted the Lord as their personal Saviour, we now began to see their faith grow. One of them, Mr Fung, shared at a Sunday meeting:

> *As you know I have one rice field that feeds my family for the year and provides a little extra income. Then last week as I was checking my field, I saw a wave of rats advancing across my neighbour's field, eating all before them. What could I do? I remembered that we are to call on God in our time of need, so I kneeled on the earth embankment between my field and my neighbour's and asked God to help me. And do you know what happened?*

The rats came to the edge of my neighbour's field, and then stopped!

It was encouraging to see the practical faith of the new believers, and we continued to support them, but we soon realised we couldn't just focus on the town. People there were friendly, but the majority were loyal to the local temple, whose monks collected alms every morning and broadcast sermons at night. Most of our friends were more interested in making money than hearing about God's plan of salvation.

However, we did find more of a welcome among the farmers, like Mr Fung, on the edge of town. Some of them began to attend the meetings in the town, and moved towards new life in Christ. As they taught us about fishing in the rice fields, their hearts gradually opened to us 'fishing for men'.

Sensing that God had still more for us in this area, we began to think of the two other districts that had been allocated to us.

6

PUSHING OUTWARDS

We had begun to realise that the people in this supposedly 'hard ground' could be reached with the gospel. Maybe, with God's help, we could break the 'mediocre' response that some in the OMF Central Thailand team had so far experienced. With the wider area of the three districts before us, Koos and I resolved to look for openings in more distant towns and villages where there were still virtually no practising Christians.

We had observed that the daytime visiting pattern practised by most missionaries was usually not very productive in villages. The people at home at that time would be children and grandparents, caring for the home, while the active – and decision-making – adults would be out in the fields. So if we were to spend quality time with the adults, we needed to be there in the evening and the early morning. However, staying overnight in different places would be costly for each of us, especially leaving our wives and children at home dealing with practical and security issues. Their full support and agreement to this was crucial.

We were initially directed to new people and places through contact cards coming from the OMF hospital at Manorom. The Christian doctors and staff regularly shared the gospel with patients and, when someone showed strong interest in Jesus or made a profession of faith, we got their details. Unfortunately, it was often very hard to track them down! Out in the villages there was no address system, so the cards used names or local landmarks. In addition, by the time we could make it out to the village, their interest had often faded. However, we kept getting cards for patients in the town of Pai Sali, 15 miles to the east of Tha Tako, so we ventured down there looking for a Mr Yuang, Mrs Jarey, and Mr Tong Juah.

Mr Yuang was not at home.

Mrs Jarey was nowhere to be found.

Mr Tong Juah could not be located, but not for want of trying.

As we motored home, it seemed like a disappointing dead end. Imagine our surprise therefore when Mr Yuang turned up at Koos' door a few days later.

'Come and visit me in Pai Sali,' Mr Yuang said. He also offered to take us to the other addresses we'd been given. So, on our second visit, we shared the gospel at Mrs Jarey's house with a small crowd of relatives and neighbours, intrigued by these foreigners who could speak their language. Sensing some real interest, we later spent a week in Mr Yuang's house with two Bible college students. During this time we also visited people around town and, in the evenings, gave slide shows and shared testimonies. By the end of the week, 10 people had confessed faith in Christ, with five others considering this step and another 10 open to receive further teaching!

We were delighted, and began a Saturday evening meeting in Pai Sali for worship, Bible teaching, and prayer. In the next few weeks, attendance grew rapidly, at one stage reaching 55 when we showed a film. Each Saturday we made evangelistic visits in the morning, before spending the evening teaching the new believers Thai worship songs and how to pray aloud. We were encouraged by how God was affirming our new approach to outreach and discipleship, but we realised we still had a lot to learn and had to remain dependent on him.

One of those who accepted the Lord in Pai Sali was Mrs Roy. Her 'way in' to God's kingdom was somewhat unusual. Mrs Roy was a gentle, middle-aged lady and a member of a strict Buddhist sect. She spent most of her time at the local temple, eating frugal meals, meditating, and seeking inner peace. But she heard the gospel when visiting her sister, Mrs Jarey. A Saviour who would provide the peace she sought attracted her and she turned to Christ.

In her Buddhist religion she had been strictly vegetarian. Having accepted Jesus as her God and creator, she now understood that she should accept the food he provided. So in front of a group of friends she ate a dish of meat curry – this was her step of faith, confirming that Jesus was now her Lord and Saviour.

As with many who turned to Christ, testing times followed. The monks tempted her to return to the temple, while many of her friends rejected her. Yet the Lord was with her and gave her a personal vision of himself. 'I just basked in his presence,' she said. She was also keen to share her new faith. Each Saturday when I visited Pai Sali, she had a list of people we should visit before the evening meeting, and many of them were open to hearing more of the gospel.

With encouraging progress in two districts, we returned to Tak Fa district. This was much less responsive, but we followed up with Mrs Arirat, who had recently become a Christian through the witness at Manorom hospital. She welcomed our visits for Bible study and prayer. Over time her husband, Taweep, saw such a change for good in his wife that he wanted to join her in the faith. This couple were among the first 20 believers we baptised in Tha Tako in November 1978 – just over a year after we had arrived in this supposedly spiritually barren place!

People's commitment to Jesus wasn't a shot in the dark either. Mrs Arirat and Taweep were fully committed in their faith and went on to establish the first church in Tak Fa town. Taweep led the church until his early death about 10 years later. The church still meets in the building he purchased, and today there are another two churches in the town.

The momentum continued. One of the members of Tha Tako church asked us to visit her relatives in Nong Mai Daeng, a village 45 minutes north of the town. Koos and I went up there and spent the evening giving a gospel presentation to a small gathering. We then talked at length to those who showed more interest. Later mosquito nets were put up and, as was now our habit, we spent the night there.

The next morning something special took place. Jesus had promised that if we followed him, he would make us 'fishers of men' (Mark 1:17, ESV). Could this be true?

We visited the homes of each of the families who had heard the gospel the previous evening. At the first house, I was led to ask, 'Would you like to accept Christ now?' The two present said 'yes'. Taking off their amulets – religious necklaces believed to have spiritual power – they prayed to confess their sin and turn to Christ.

Sensing God was leading us onwards, we went to the second house and I asked the same question. This time three people prayed for salvation. Encouraged by the Lord, we returned to our host's house and asked the question once more. This time four people prayed to receive Christ. In one day, a new church had been born with nine members!

Soon these new Christians were meeting regularly and growing in Christ. Usually they would meet after their day's work in the fields. After a meal they would sit in a circle on the smooth wooden floor, by the light of a few spluttering oil lamps. Then they would read the Bible, sing hymns, pray for each other, and share how God had helped them since the last meeting.

The Lord continued to work through us with another baptism service on Easter Sunday 1979. Twenty-five people were baptised in the river just outside Tha Tako and were received with warm words and dry towels. More singing followed, celebrating this expression of new life in Christ. Sitting on the bank, trying to get some shade, I quietly gave thanks for all that God had done over the last 18 months. He had brought 45 people to confess their faith in baptism, and had given them a hunger to keep growing in their walk with him and a love for each other and for us.

My thoughts were interrupted by a commotion among the small crowd of onlookers on the bridge over the river. Among their number were a few of the local monks. They had noticed two Western families among the Thai believers. When they realised that fellow Thai people had embraced a foreign faith, they believed they had just witnessed an act of betrayal – as we soon discovered.

The next morning, posters had appeared on the roadside trees denouncing the new Christians as those fooled by foreigners into betraying their own people and religion. Excited groups around town began talking of demonstrations, violence, and getting the foreigners out. While some of the Christians went to meet the ringleaders and the hostility began to lessen, a group of townspeople took matters into their own hands. They began to march towards our house, armed with a hand grenade and not afraid to use it.

Along the way they happened to pass the home of Mrs Pon, one of the new Christians. She bravely confronted them and asked what they were doing.

'Eliminating the threat to our nation,' they told her.

'Christians are taught to love their nation and pray for the king,' she responded. 'Come and see!' Mrs Pon invited them to come up into her house and showed them her framed picture of the king on the wall.

'Oh, we didn't realise you are loyal,' they admitted, and agreed to call off their mission.

We only heard about this near miss the following day, and gave thanks for the Lord's protection and all he had done through us so far. God's kingdom was growing in Tha Tako, but would this growth continue? And could we disciple these new believers through the testing times that would surely come their way?

7

BUILDING COMMUNITY

Our focused outreach programme in the first 18 months now gave way to a steady forward movement. We were aware that the Christian community must not be dependent on the energies of a missionary team, but rather on the mutual support that the believers gave to one another. In this way faith could grow, members would feel at home in the church meetings and festivals, and the gospel would continue to flow forth. We were learning from the early church, where 'all the believers were together … and ate together with glad and sincere hearts' (Acts 2:44, 46).

The need for such a mutually supportive community was underlined when we suffered a health setback. Jenny developed severe dysentery, which lasted several weeks and left her weak and listless. After getting over this, a few months later she contracted dengue fever. This caused a very high temperature and pain over all her body, with ice packs and paracetamol our only resources! Jenny's condition slowly improved, but weeks of depression followed.

While caring for Jenny, my contribution to the work was reduced. But at this time our team began to grow. We were joined in Tha Tako by Thai co-workers Mr Wicharn and Mr Pyrote and their families. They had recently finished Bible college in north Thailand and needed a placement to try out their newly learned ministry skills. Their contribution in leading meetings and visiting the believers was particularly helpful. They also helped demonstrate what a Thai Christian family should look like in an area with few role models.

The value of the small groups worshipping together had been apparent from the beginning, but now we wanted the wider community of Christians to come together for mutual encouragement and to establish a public identity together. One of our first ventures was a joint Christmas celebration. In December 1978 believers from every group gathered at Mr Yuang's large house in Pai Sali and greatly enjoyed the time together, sharing worship, many hilarious games, and a delicious feast.

Following this, on the first Sunday of each month we held a joint meeting for all the believers from the three districts. They came together for a day of worship and fellowship, alternating between Tha Tako and Pai Sali. Normally we invited a preacher from outside the district and celebrated communion together. These regular meetings not only built the believers' faith, but also established their identity together as the people of God, giving them confidence in their Christian lives.

Another important part of forming a new Christian community concerned the area of marriage. In Thai culture parents generally arranged marriages, but we wanted to ensure Christians married within the faith – for the sake of not just the believers themselves, but also the future health of the church. One difficulty was that Christian young people were often the only single person in their group. The monthly combined meetings gave an opportunity for the young people to meet, and I was also able to do some matchmaking between people from different groups!

In 1980 Mr Deng and Miss Teo, believers from different villages, became the first Christian couple to marry in the area. The day before the ceremony, believers from around the region arrived at Teo's family home and started to transform it into a suitable wedding venue. They set up sound systems, prepared food, and made floral decorations from locally gathered foliage and flowers. Elaborate garlands were woven for the bride and groom, and one wall was covered with a large cloth, with the names of bride and groom in large polystyrene letters across the middle.

Only about half of the 80-strong congregation were Christians; the rest were curious neighbours, interested to see what a Christian wedding would look like. Mr Wicharn and Mr Pyrote conducted the ceremony, while I led the singing on my guitar. Missionary colleagues put garlands round the necks of the bride and groom. The service set the pattern for future Christian weddings in the area – we were forming Christian traditions as we went along!

Funerals were quite a different challenge. One critical question Thai people asked before becoming Christians was what would be provided in the event of their death. Local funerals usually lasted a week, culminating in a procession to the temple for the cremation. Preparing for one's death was an important task long before the event.

So what would be provided for a Christian funeral in the area? If there was no Christian alternative, the body would have to be cremated at a Buddhist temple. For many potential converts this could be a barrier to them accepting the Christian way, so we sought to make what preparations we could.

Our first funeral took place in May 1980, with the death of Mrs Guan in Nong Mai Daeng. She was one of the original nine believers there and had been baptised in April 1979. For several weeks her health deteriorated, which gave time to prepare for her eventual departure.

We had a coffin made and booked the OMF Land Rover to use as a hearse. Having located a Roman Catholic cemetery in Nakhon Sawan, we obtained permission to use a plot there. 'You will have to dig the grave yourselves,' we were told, so several of the Thai believers volunteered for the task and spent a couple of days digging the hole.

The day Mrs Guan died, the believers from Tha Tako drove up to Nong Mai Daeng, crossing a field to get to her house. The coffin was draped with a cloth and all was ready for the evening ceremony. But about 6 p.m. the heavens opened and we had several hours of torrential rain. The noise on the roof was so great that the ceremony had to be postponed until the following morning.

When it was time to move the coffin after the ceremony, the previously dry field was now under six inches of water! The Land Rover-turned-hearse only got a few yards through the sea of mud before becoming stuck.

Some of the locals came to watch, and mockingly observed that we would have to return to the temple in the end.

Help came in an unexpected way. One of the church members had a tractor, which he used to winch the Land Rover and cars across the field. Further on, though abandoned buses blocked the entry road, somehow we got through. We arrived at the graveside by mid-afternoon, and all gave thanks not only for Mrs Guan's life, but also for a successful burial.

We were conscious that the Lord had led us as we continued to lay the foundations for the newly emerging Christian community.

Besides important occasions like weddings and funerals, day-to-day discipleship was a growing challenge as the number of disciples continued to increase. How were the Christians in their different villages to grow in faith when we were able to spend so little personal time with them? Being a rural community, many struggled to read the Bibles that were available. But then a boost came from the latest 1980s technology. Battery cassette tape players were now available locally, and I realised these could be an effective discipleship tool for individuals and groups to listen to together. We ordered 25 and distributed them to key households. I made recordings of Thai preachers speaking at conferences and obtained material from a Christian radio station. I also discovered a dramatised version of the Old Testament and recordings of the songs in our Thai hymn book. I then scrounged used cassettes from missionaries, as well as purchasing many new ones. Eventually I had a catalogue of over 100 different master recordings available, and made these into sets of tapes, which believers could swap week by week.

Mrs Roy, one of the early believers, was not a fast reader, having left school many years earlier. But her knowledge of Christian doctrine and Bible stories was considerable thanks to these tapes. She spent many hours a week ironing clothes for her family and for neighbours, and her main companion during that time was the cassette player. She told me happily, 'If I'm unclear after one play through, I just run it through again!'

Through the tapes and the mutual encouragement of fellow believers, the Christians continued to grow in faith, even when we couldn't visit them.

The community of Thai believers was a real source of joy. But at the same time there were concerns. The failure of some to live the Christian life could destroy the testimony of the newly formed church. Mrs Roy's sister, Mrs Jarey, was among the first to turn to Christ in Pai Sali. We learned – accidentally, through conversation with another believer – that since then Mrs Jarey had continued her work as a prostitute, involving some of her daughters as well.

When we went to see her, she said that she could not and would not give up her present work – she needed the income. She also 'felt sorry' for her regular customers. Sadly we couldn't find a way forward. So, with regret, she stopped professing to be a Christian and returned her Bible. It was a real discouragement.

During the next few years, though, her customers tailed off, and eventually the last one died. Mrs Jarey then expressed genuine repentance and wanted to return to the Christian faith. She prayed for forgiveness and cleansing, and requested her Bible back. She went on to become an evangelist and later a keen Sunday school teacher with a testimony of God's grace to her.

Not all these cases had a good ending, but in each situation we looked to the Lord to guide us. The promise

'I will instruct you and teach you in the way you should go' (Psalm 32:8) was a great encouragement. We were so privileged to be part of the church God was building in rural Thailand.

8

FACING TESTING!

Though we liked our little house on stilts in Tha Tako, we hadn't realised that, being close to the rice fields, it could be flooded in the rainy season. One day we returned from an overnight stay in Manorom to find the house standing in three feet of water. But that was no problem, we thought, since upstairs was dry – although we would have to go to the market in the small boats locals used.

After the flood water had dried up, I began cleaning out my small office, built between the pillars under the house. I started to remove some items from shelving that had been above the water level. One of these was a tall metal tin that I used for a wastepaper basket. Taking it down, I began to gather some of the paper that was still in there, only to uncover the round form of a coiled snake.

With an involuntary jerk I dropped the tin – which fortunately landed away from me – and out leapt the shining form of a cobra! It immediately reared up, with its hooded face confronting me, blocking the way between me and the door.

Realising that my hand had been an inch from the cobra's head, I was glued to the spot in a cold sweat. After a cobra bite you have just two hours to live, unless an antidote can be given. And the nearest hospital was at least two hours away.

Slowly I backed away from the cobra, which was still standing between me and the door. Happily there was a window at the side. I carefully climbed out, and then shut the door on the snake.

A neighbour was not far away, so we called for help. With hardly a thought she killed it, and took it away for making 'snake medicine'.

As we gave thanks for God's protection, we realised even more how dependent we were on him for our physical safety and care.

Not all our testing was physical. The world of evil spirits, though strange to us as Westerners, was part of everyday life for our Thai friends. Their constant aim was to appease the spirits, whether that was on their person with amulets and tattoos, or in their homes with offerings placed on various spirit shelves. As a result demonic activity was widely present.

One day I was at the home of an old lady who made her living by skinning and cooking field rats for sale. She was open to the gospel, so I visited her from time to time. On this visit we were sitting on the wooden floor of her house-on-stilts when a young woman, a relative of the lady, came up the steps and joined us. 'I have two problems,' she shared. 'One is that I am constantly unwell. Another is that my father, who died two years ago, is speaking to me and urging me to kill myself to come and join him. What shall I do?'

With no previous experience of this, I was learning 'on the job'! The Holy Spirit led me to reply that no father who loved his daughter would urge suicide like this. I told her that the voice she was hearing was not that of her father, but a demon impersonating him. I then asked permission to pray for her.

First I bound the demon in the name of Jesus, commanding it to leave. Then I prayed for her healing. Finally I prayed that God would open her heart to believe in his Son, the Lord Jesus Christ.

A week later she came to the old lady's house again. She reported that she was free of the demon's oppression, that her physical pain had lifted, and that now she wanted to believe in Jesus. 'My throat was constricted by the demon last week,' she shared, 'so I could not pray aloud.' I was then able to lead her in a simple prayer accepting Jesus as her Saviour and Lord.

Subsequently the girl moved back to her home province in northeast Thailand, and I never saw her again. But word to the old lady reported that six months later she continued in her new faith. I was encouraged to see firsthand the authority of the Lord Jesus over the demonic world – which would be helpful in other cases I would meet in the future.

Physical and emotional trials also hit the lives of those who were turning to Christ. For example, in Nong Mai Daeng village, where the Lord had earlier worked so amazingly to start a church of nine members in one day, the believers had been sharing their faith with Mr Pot. He was one of the more aggressive characters in the village, but before long both he and his wife accepted the Lord and welcomed us warmly into their home. That he was a changed man was clear from the fact he gave up stealing and began giving to others instead.

Then Mr Pot told us about his son, Nurome, who was far more lawless than his father had been. Nurome was part of a band of robbers who had killed several people in the previous few years and had recently killed again. His Christian cousin had often witnessed to him, but now Nurome was lying in a Bangkok hospital, fighting for his life, having been knifed in a brawl.

Koos and I needed to go to Bangkok, so offered to visit him there. After much searching, we found Nurome in a hospital bed, looking yellow and very poorly. We shared the gospel with him and encouraged him to believe. We then prayed with him that God would touch his life, and save both his body and his soul.

Returning to Tha Tako, we sent word to Mr Pot to get ready for a funeral. This young man clearly had only a few days to live.

Two days later, however, Nurome felt that he had been miraculously healed. He unhooked his drips, discharged himself from hospital, and boarded a bus heading north. Several hours and a three-mile walk across the fields later, he arrived home, announced that he was now believing in Christ, and asked when the next church meeting was. Clearly our faith was lacking.

Physical and spiritual opposition to the work was such an everyday experience that we almost grew to expect it. Sometimes it seemed as if even the elements were against us. But promises such as 'Blessed is the one who perseveres under trial' (James 1:12) were a great encouragement, and helped us to keep going.

For example, our baptism service in October 1980 almost didn't happen. A week of torrential rain had turned the dirt roads into slimy mud. On the Wednesday before the service, we wondered if the baptism candidates could still travel. We were concerned particularly for two of them – Mr Pot's daughter, Aree, and her husband, Prayune – who were living in Nong Mai Daeng village, a half-hour journey to the north. Wicharn and I decided to visit them to confirm arrangements.

After struggling up the partially flooded road to Nong Mai Daeng, we discovered that the couple were working in a village some way further north. It was agreed that

Aree's younger brother, Nurome, now fully recovered, would go with us as a guide.

The gravel road alternated between smooth, dry sections and wet, slippery stretches where the bikes occasionally spun sideways, and we had to use our feet to keep them upright. The road then branched northeast and got progressively worse, becoming sticky mud cut into deep troughs by tractor tyres. We drove along these troughs, twisting and turning to keep upright, but occasionally plunging down two or three feet into deep gouged-out holes. Our arms and legs began to ache.

Eventually we reached a crossroads only to be told that the normal three-mile route was blocked, but we could try a nine-mile detour. So for the next two hours, we battled, lunged, and slithered our way round the detour, finding we were having to ride in flooded sections of road. The bikes began to cut out in the water and were only restarted with difficulty. Then it rained!

After five and a half hours of travel with our guide, we reached another crossroads, only about two miles from our destination. We were weak, bruised, aching all over, with hands numb from the hours of gripping the handlebars. And the last stretch was absolutely impassable. It was a sea of deep mud as far as the eye could see. So now what?

Nurome said, 'You can't stay here – there are too many bandits. You can't go home the way we came – you wouldn't make it. You must return a better way. I'll stay here and walk in to find Prayune and Aree. I'll stay with them.'

After such an ordeal we weren't going to see our friends at all. And now many hours of travel along unknown, possibly dangerous and difficult roads lay ahead. So trusting it all into the Lord's hands, we left Nurome and set off for home.

After a further three-hours' nerve-wracking riding, we finally arrived back in Tha Tako, just as night was falling. By that stage Wicharn was riding one-handed; the other, numb from hours of holding on tight, was now tucked into his shirt. Both of us were on the point of collapse. In fact, Wicharn developed a fever, and was only just okay again in time for the Sunday meeting four days later. Had the whole trip been a complete waste of time and energy?

Sunday morning saw us gather for worship, with Wicharn leading the service and me in the congregation. None of those we had gone to find had shown up. As Wicharn continued to lead the meeting, suddenly his face broke into a huge smile. The 60 or so people gathered there all turned round, and we saw Nurome come in, followed by Prayune and Aree.

The couple had heard about our struggles to reach them and determined to make every effort to get to the service. It took a day to finish up their work, then the next day they trekked five hours through the mud, before catching a bus to Nong Mai Daeng. 'And today at last we've made it to Tha Tako!' they smiled.

Later that day Nurome, Aree, and Prayune were all baptised with several others at the edge of a flooded rice field, witnessed by the church. Each one spoke and testified to the work of God in their hearts, and of their desire to live for him. How good is the God we adore, who does not disappoint his children in their times of trial!

9

ATTACKS WITHOUT CEASING

Miss Lawt was among the first believers we baptised in Tha Tako, back in November 1978. She was in her mid-twenties and lived on her parents' farm in the village of Damrongrak, on the southern road to Tak Fa. She had come to faith a few years earlier at the OMF hospital in Manorom, but with no contact with other Christians, she was barely hanging on to her faith. After our visits to encourage her, she had taken the step of baptism. A few years later, her witness to her friends and relatives was beginning to bear fruit, and several of them came to faith.

A regular Christian meeting was started in her village in early 1981, and other friends began to attend. Among these was a young man called Yothin, nephew of the chief monk at the local Buddhist temple. Before long, Yothin decided to become a Christian, to the great fury of his uncle.

Almost immediately Yothin's uncle took action and stirred up the whole community to ostracise and threaten the Christians. He also issued death threats against the OMF team members if we continued to visit the village. We knew this was not an idle warning. Violent killings were commonplace in the area, and the local police struggled to provide protection and uphold the law.

So we stopped visiting the village and also avoided travelling alone on the roads if we could. But we also knew we could trust each day to the Lord's sovereign care. The Christians in the village moved to work elsewhere for a time, but Lawt remained, still strong in her faith. The Tha Tako believers prayed constantly for the area, looking for opportunity to visit again.

This prayer was answered. They had learned the truth that 'Your enemy the devil prowls around like a roaring lion' but that in Christ they could 'resist him' (1 Peter 5:8–9). After several weeks, some of the Thai believers took courage and went to visit and speak to the village headman. He assured them it was now safe for us to return. We praised God for the change and for restoring to us an open door for the gospel.

On our return, as well as encouraging the Damrongrak Christians, we wanted to talk to Lawt about marriage. She had procrastinated for years as to who she should marry, and it was invaluable for her to talk to Jenny about what Christian marriage meant.

In recent months Lawt had got to know Chai, a young Christian man from Nong Mai Daeng, and there seemed to be a spiritual affinity as well as mutual attraction there. He had indicated his interest in her, and understanding was growing. But he also wasn't too sure what Christian marriage involved, so I spent time with him, helping him understand not just the joys but the responsibilities of marriage. Eventually all was agreed, and he and Lawt became engaged.

The wedding was arranged for 12 May 1981. Lawt took the bold step of preparing wedding invitations to take to everyone in the village, especially those who had ostracised her in the past. To Lawt's surprise, the majority said they would be delighted to attend! Perhaps they were curious to see what a Christian wedding would look like; maybe they were intrigued by the courageous testimony of this young woman.

The ceremony took place in Lawt's home, and most of the villagers attended, including the village headman and the school headmaster, another key figure in the village. The opposition of just months earlier seemed to have disappeared, and the presence of a Christian family in Damrongrak was now being celebrated. Chai and Lawt continued to be faithful servants of the Lord, and several years later were still encouraging the local believers in Damrongrak. How good and faithful is our God.

Meanwhile, the weight of responsibility for the work had continued to grow. Apart from follow-up visits and evangelism, weekly meetings were now being held in six locations. With the new believers having little Bible knowledge, we tried to have a team member present at each of these meetings.

For some time Koos had been experiencing physical exhaustion, so he and the family took early home assignment, leaving for Canada in July 1980. This was a major loss to the team as Koos and I had worked closely together right from the beginning.

Then in December 1980 one of our Thai co-workers, Mr Pyrote, left to gain further ministry experience in south Thailand. Naturally I was pleased to still have Wicharn with us. But then he was invited to take up a position with World Vision, so left by February 1981. Just Jenny and I were left virtually alone to care for the work of outreach and caring for believers.

How were we to cope? Was God still sovereign over our situation? Jenny and I now looked to the Lord in prayer for his help. Step by step we saw it arrive.

It had long been our aim for the believers to take more responsibility for their own groups. Now they needed to do so, earlier than expected. So I appointed a leader in each group, both to care for the members and to lead local meetings as needed. In order that the leaders were encouraged, they came to each of the monthly combined meetings for discussion and prayer.

The arrival of new team members – Koos' brother, Bill, and his wife, Lois – was also a great help. They had recently joined OMF Thailand, and despite having little Thai language and church-planting experience, they agreed to help us. Bill was keen to see the work progress, and we worked well together.

Though still a small team, we aimed to provide as much pastoral visiting and Bible ministry as possible. Jenny and Lois also joined Bill and me on the road when the children were away at boarding school. With women being in the majority in both the Nong Mai Daeng and Pai Sali groups, it was particularly valuable for Jenny to spend time with them, and they were able to share things I was not permitted to hear!

By July 1981 it was time for us to return to the UK for our home assignment. Since arriving in Tha Tako in 1977 we now had seen 72 people baptised, including six at our most recent baptisms. God had continued to work wonderfully despite all the setbacks.

At the monthly combined meeting held just before we left, it was wonderful to be surrounded by all our new brothers and sisters in Christ as they prayed for Jenny, Hannah, Paul, and me. They urged us to return and continue the work – there was still so much to be done!

It was hard to leave, but it helped knowing that Koos and Colleen were on their way back to Tha Tako after their home assignment in Canada. We met them briefly in the OMF mission home in Bangkok, Koos now fully recovered from his exhaustion. They were so excited to be returning to Tha Tako, knowing there was so much potential in the church there, and we were excited to see what God would do through them.

10

VALLEY OF THE SHADOW

On Sunday 25 October 1981 I was preaching at a small church in Shropshire. We had been back in the UK for three months, updating our prayer supporters about the work in Thailand. After the service there was a phone call for me from Jenny. She had just received a message from the OMF UK office that Koos had been shot dead the previous evening.

I could hardly believe it. Stunned by the news, I returned home to Manchester and then, on the Monday, headed to London, where I was doing extra studies at London Bible College. With the encouragement of OMF colleagues also studying there, I decided to make a short visit back to Thailand.

Arriving in Bangkok two days later, I first spent time with Koos' widow, Colleen, his brother, Bill, and his wife, Lois, sharing our deep grief together. We visited the Protestant cemetery, where Koos had been buried the previous day in the 'OMF corner', where over the years many of our fellow workers had also been buried.

The following day I took the 150-mile bus ride northwards to Tha Tako, arriving about noon. In the meeting place there, I spent several hours with a steady stream of believers coming to see me. Many were our hugs and tears as we comforted one another, and all were encouraged in a new commitment to follow and serve the Lord.

The last bus that night took me 15 miles eastwards to Pai Sali, the nearest town to the village where Koos had been killed. Within a few minutes many of the Pai Sali believers gathered, and here there seemed to be an even greater work of God taking place. The Christians not only showed much care towards me, but consoled me in saying that Koos had not died in vain. They said they were all prepared to die for the faith, and in fact loved the Lord more than ever.

I wrote to the OMF leaders at the time:

> *The whole church here seemed to have been raised to a new spiritual plane, and people who were backsliders or opponents of the gospel only four months ago were now sitting praising the Lord. During our impromptu meeting many testimonies were given of the Lord's working in their lives subsequent to Koos' death. Despite some mocking from outsiders, they spoke of unparalleled opportunities given to share their faith with others.*

I soon heard more of what had happened to Koos. On the day of the shooting, a group of the Pai Sali Christians were going to the village of Khao Din, where a new group had been started. Despite feeling tired that evening, Koos had felt 'inwardly compelled' to go. After the meeting he went to the house where they were staying, and joined a circle of the believers chatting about the spiritual needs of the group. Five minutes later a single shotgun cartridge was fired from a gun pushed through the woven bamboo fence. It hit Koos in the lower half of the face and neck, causing him to die instantly.

Once I was back in Tha Tako, the group leaders called a meeting and invited me to join them. They shared that they would not lose heart and committed themselves to 'fill the gap' left by Koos' departure, leading and caring for the groups as best they could. They also agreed to invite Mr Pyrote, our former co-worker in the town, to return from south Thailand and help with the spiritual harvest now expected.

The love of Christ continued to impact the believers in Pai Sali. That Saturday evening they took gifts of food and words of forgiveness to the man arrested for Koos' murder in Pai Sali jail. He was moved to tears by their care.

My visit was drawing to a close, but first the monthly combined morning worship meeting was to be held in Tha Tako for believers from the four centres. The response was overwhelming, with almost 120 filling the Tha Tako meeting house. I was asked to preach, and reminded them that 'our Lord Almighty reigns' (Revelation 19:6).

All people are to know him and make him known, as Koos did during his life. The warmth of their response was overwhelming, and they reaffirmed their invitation for my family and me to return.

I travelled back to the UK deeply moved by all I had seen and heard. I reflected on how the evil one had overreached himself. Instead of hindering the work of God's kingdom in the region, Koos' death had been used by the Lord to strengthen it.

11

GOING DOWN AND GOING UP

'Do we really want to come back here?' we wondered, as we made our way back to Tha Tako in June 1982. Just eight months after Koos' death, Jenny was understandably afraid that she might also become a widow like Colleen. After all, I would be visiting many of the areas where Koos had been, and his killer was still out there. The man who had initially been arrested for the murder had been released without charge, with no case against him being upheld. Remarkably I didn't have that same fear, rather just a deep sense of the need to press on with what God had given us to do, despite everything.

I did have a heaviness of heart, however, for a different reason. The initial spiritual uplift of the believers in the wake of Koos' death seemed not to have lasted. Meetings for worship and Bible study were poorly attended – the 20-strong Tha Tako town group now had only eight attending. Some of the believers had gone back to their old ways, even going to the temple, or were behaving inappropriately. How could this have happened? It appeared that the evil one had been active in our absence.

Positively it was good to learn that Mr Pyrote, who had gone to south Thailand 18 months earlier, had now returned to Tha Tako. He soon realised the deterioration that had taken place and got in touch with Mr Snguan, one of the church leaders. They began meeting for an hour each day to pray for the welfare of the church.

During the next two months, Pyrote and I visited different believers, providing spiritual 'check-ups'. Many sins were acknowledged, including adultery, stealing, wrong financial dealings, jealousies, and slander. Prayers of confession and the receiving of forgiveness usually followed.

In our preaching we looked at some of the passages dealing with the moral failures of God's people. On one occasion when Pyrote was preaching, he named six major sins from 1 Corinthians 5:11: being 'sexually immoral or greedy, an idolater or slanderer, a drunkard or swindler'. He knew that the influence of the temple and the brothel were very close at hand. He then invited those who had done these things to stand. Many responded, but after prayer for repentance and forgiveness, there was an atmosphere of relief and joy! I wondered if we were returning to a time of revived faith, and prayed that it might be so. To consolidate this upsurge of spiritual life, it was vital that effective pastoral care was provided for the believers – in addition to further outreach. The Lord helped us in several ways. First, now that our children were at boarding school, Jenny – together with Pyrote's wife, Yupin – was able to make many home visits to the women.

Also, although Bill and Lois were no longer with us, our missionary team began to grow again. Steve and Holly Niphakis, Lloyd and Darlene Oppel, and Les Williamson, all from North America, joined us. They were keen and full of new ideas. Steve soon built a trolley to sell Christian books to people waiting for their buses in Tha Tako. Over in Pai Sali, the Oppels' house became the venue for a regular Sunday worship meeting.

To build a good faith-foundation for the believers, we introduced a 'Home Bible Seminary' course, which aimed to take students through the whole Bible in five years. Participants were so excited about what they were learning in the weekly sessions that they went on to teach others who couldn't attend. To further strengthen their faith, members were encouraged to join with us in evangelistic outreach, and we started up again film shows round the villages.

As with the early church, the Lord continued to confirm his word with 'signs following'. It was about this time that the unexpected encounter with assassin-cum-builder Mr Gram took place. With several of his relatives also coming to faith, there was now a regular fellowship meeting in his village, close to Tha Tako.

Fifteen miles to the east, in Pai Sali, the Lord was also powerfully at work. One Sunday morning, part way through the morning service at the Oppels' house, a disturbance brought the meeting to a halt. Three strangers were at the door asking whether this was the place where the true God was worshipped.

It transpired that two of the men had been bringing their friend back from hospital in the city of Nakhon Sawan when he went into a coma and seemed to have died. This was a negative reaction to a penicillin injection in hospital. While the men were wondering what to do next, their 'dead' friend woke up! He then asked, 'Where is the meeting where they worship the true God?'

The friend said he had experienced his spirit leaving his body and going upwards. He then was apprehended by an angel who told him to return to his body. He was told, 'Go and join some Thai Christians in this town who are presently worshipping the true God.'

So the three arrived at the door of the meeting place, mystified at what had happened. The believers, initially astonished at this divine intervention, were delighted at this addition to their numbers and were assured that God was truly with them.

People were being revived – physically and spiritually – and the larger team was reaching out in each of the regional districts. At the same time, the leadership of the churches in the Tha Tako area decided it was time to consider

David walking in the Lake District with Senior Scouts 1960.

David and Jenny newly married in London, about to start at London Bible College in September 1969.

David, Jenny and Hannah ▸ in Bangkok in 1972.

◂ The party of new OMF workers in Thailand in 1973. Top: Koos Fietje, Martina De Wit, David with Paul. Second row: Jenny, Grace Pettigrew, Colleen Fietje, Hannah, Michael Fietje.

David in Chainat with his home-made book trolley on his way to sell Christian books at the market in 1974.

David with the members of the new Christian group he started in Taak Faa, 1975.

David staying overnight for evening meeting in Nong Mai Deng village, 1980. It was at these evening meetings that people often made decisions for Christ. As described in Chapter 6, it was in this village that a church had started dramatically with nine people turning to Jesus in just one evening.

David, Jenny, Hannah and Paul in Tha Tako just after the Christians there have prayed for them ahead of returning to the UK for home assignment in July 1981.

David and family with Bill and Lois Fietje, welcoming Koos and Colleen Fietje and family back to Thailand after Koos' and Colleen's home assignment. This was the last time David would see Koos alive.

Jenny getting to know the neighbours in Tha Tako, 1983.

David in Bangkok meeting with local church leaders, 1992.

David with the small OMF team that welcomed him to Cambodia in 1995.

◂ David outside the new church plant at Pochentong, 1999.

Mary, now a key team member, joins David on a visit to Kratie, early 2002.

David and Mary outside the newly built Team Centre in Phnom Penh in 2002.

The OMF Cambodia team in 2003, 85 members from 17 countries.

David and Mary at one of the many Thai Fellowship groups in the UK.

UK Thai believers Fellowship Weekend at a Scout hut in Manchester, 2019.

Attendees at the annual four day camp for UK Thai Christians, 2023.

David and Mary ▶ in the Lake District, 2022.

having a church building. Rather than continuing to use the mission home, now too small and only a temporary solution, the believers wanted a place that secured their identity as a Christian body in the town. They would build the church themselves.

Suitable land was found, funds were raised, and the purchase made. As it was a rice field, it needed 80 lorry loads of dirt to level it. After a year's wait for the land to settle, construction could begin. Members carried out the work under the direction of ex-builder-cum-assassin Mr Gram. He told the members what to do, how to dig foundations, how to prepare metal for the upright concrete posts, and how to mix the cement.

Their commitment was impressive, and different groups came to lend a hand. From time to time the money ran out, stopping the work, and days of prayer were held. Funds enabled the work to continue, the walls to be built, and the wooden roof trusses to be placed. But then a crisis came – there was no money for the tiles, meaning the wood would soon bend and be useless.

A church in Canada, not knowing the situation, happened to allocate their annual missionary offering to church work in Thailand. It reached Tha Tako just in time. Roof tiles were purchased and fitted, and a beautiful Thai 'two-level' roofing style took shape.

The building could now be used – high walls and extra rooms would have to wait for another day. All was ready in time for Easter Sunday 1985. Many believers from Tha Tako and elsewhere joined to give thanks for the building and to consecrate it to the glory of God.

When we arrived in Tha Tako in 1977, there were no Christians and no churches in the area. We had learned and experienced so much, both from our earlier church-planting efforts in Chai Nat and now in this challenging area. Despite often feeling weak and inadequate, we had grown in faith and obedience to God's leading, especially in how to gather and disciple people. As we looked back, we were amazed at how the Lord had worked through us and our colleagues over the last eight years to establish three thriving town churches, one with its own building. Over this missionary term we had also seen 39 people baptised. Adding these to those from our first term made a total of 111 believers baptised in all. Most of these were standing firm, though a few had fallen away.

We were now in our final six months in Tha Tako. As we knew we would be assigned to a different ministry in our next term of service, this was an especially precious time. We had moved to live in the market house, where the meetings had originally been held, which gave us a good opportunity to welcome visitors. Many believers who we had formerly sought out in distant villages now came to visit us instead. There were many opportunities to talk through different aspects of their Christian lives.

On 22 July 1985 Jenny spoke at her final ladies' meeting there. All were moved by her talk about the love of the Lord Jesus and how it had upheld her during these recent years in Tha Tako. The ladies sang special songs for her, and tears flowed freely.

The following day I preached for the last time at the Tha Tako meeting. My message was 'Don't forget the grace of God that has come to you all in the Lord Jesus.'

It was difficult to leave, so surrounded by love and good wishes, but we were mindful of the promise 'you know that your labour in the Lord is not in vain' (1 Corinthians 15:58). Such was our heart emotion as we left for the UK.

12

NEW DOORS OPEN

During most of our home assignment in the UK, we were excited at the prospect of moving to a new ministry. We would be overseeing throughout the central Thailand region the Home Bible Study programme we had used in Tha Tako. Then we received a letter from the OMF Thailand Field Director. The team leader for central Thailand had unexpectedly needed to return to New Zealand. Would we fill the role for six months?

Until now I had deliberately avoided getting involved in team leadership, preferring to focus on church planting. But we sensed the invitation was from the Lord. So, with some trepidation, we set out for Takhli, the home and office of the central Thailand field leader, in June 1986.

That concern was well founded. The office was in the style of 'everything everywhere', the whereabouts of any papers known only to the previous occupant. Not only that, but half the data needed was on the office computer. I had never used a computer, and found the equipment unplugged, with no idea how to set it up. But by examining the dust marks on each of the plugs, I was able to 'guess' them back into their rightful slots, and now we could get started!

A whirlwind six months followed. From dealing with team issues that had been put on hold until I arrived, to getting new workers set up and serving, my hands were full. I found I had to care for a 35-strong team of missionaries in 16 towns across an area the size of Wales.

We knew that our colleagues needed all the encouragement they could get. Church growth in central Thailand had been slow. Although OMF had been working in the region for 35 years, by 1986 there were still less than 1000 believers. Momentum had recently begun to increase, and we were keen to sustain that. So, joined by Jenny wherever possible, I resolved to visit each of the ministry stations in turn in the first two-month period, and to try and visit regularly after that.

We much enjoyed our visits with team members, aiming to put creative work arrangements in place. As they shared the joys and difficulties they were facing, we found what we had learned in Tha Tako could help them be more fruitful in their ministry. Jenny and I also did some local church ministry. Occasionally we headed up north to Tha Tako, including for the official opening of the completed church building on 19 July 1986.

By January 1987 the team leader had returned and it was time for us to move on. We hoped our time 'holding the fort' had been useful and encouraged our colleagues in their work – we had certainly learned a lot about the responsibilities of leadership. We now arranged to move elsewhere in central Thailand to begin our work with the Home Bible Study programme. Prior to that we were due a month's language refresher in Bangkok.

We had only been in Bangkok a few days when our plans changed again! The OMF Bangkok team leader unexpectedly had to return to Australia, and would we take over as acting team leader for three months?

Though taken by surprise, we sensed this was God's plan for us, and so were ready to accept the new role. This seemed yet another 'open door' that God had placed before us (Revelation 3:8). However, life in Thailand's capital was very different to the rural life we were used to. We had a lot to learn.

In the first month, I visited the three OMF church plants in Bangkok, sorted out the team finances, and unscrambled a host of team issues. I even drove the OMF General Director, James Hudson Taylor III, from the airport to central Thailand! My busy first month seemed a reflection of the pace of life in the dusty city, with a seemingly unending flow of people and traffic, and the relentless heat reflecting off the buildings.

Church planting was only a small part of OMF's work in Bangkok. The majority of the OMF team members were serving in support ministries – publishing, Christian radio, Bible college teaching, student outreach, refugee work, and a rescue ministry for exploited girls. We found we were also responsible for Study House, the centre for new missionary arrivals, as well as the OMF holiday home at Hua Hin, 200 miles south of Bangkok.

With such diverse ministries, an early priority was to build a coherent team. We had learned in our first few years in Thailand how the enemy aimed to divide the Lord's servants and undermine open fellowship between colleagues. I therefore introduced a monthly prayer meeting for everyone and a joint prayer letter, and these began to strengthen our team unity.

Jenny was responsible for running Study House – a daunting task of its own. This involved caring for between 10 and 15 new missionaries at any time. Their accommodation, meals, projects, and guided activities – everything apart from their attendance at language school – were all arranged by Jenny, a role she enjoyed and flourished in.

After the initial three months as team leaders, we were asked to continue in the position for the next three years. We were happy to be asked and agreed, but wondered if we could cope. With a growing mountain of administrative tasks, we needed somehow to maintain our own health and sanity. Living in the Study House compound, we were permanently on duty and at the call of the team and new workers!

We implemented several strategies to help sustain us long-term. Saturdays were designated as our 'day off', which gave opportunity for time together, often while eating ice cream in one of the big hotels! We prioritised a solid spiritual life, and were much in prayer for the many challenges before us. I formed a Field Council to help manage team affairs, relieving some of the pressure. As Bible ministry begun to open up, we could enjoy fellowship with the local Christian community.

In August 1987 I attended the annual meeting of the Associated Churches of Thailand in central Thailand. This was a group of churches that had been planted by OMF workers over the last 35 years. Church associations from north, central, and south Thailand, and tribal groups were represented. But to my dismay there was no association for the capital city.

Back in Bangkok I spoke to the three OMF-supported churches, to see if they wanted to link together for support and fellowship. There wasn't much enthusiasm for the idea, as most of them didn't know each other. Then an opportunity to bring the churches together presented itself. Operation Mobilisation's ship *Logos* was about to visit the docks in Bangkok. So I invited a group from each of the churches to visit the ship at the same time, and then brought them together in the ship's lounge.

Ajarn Narin, a church leader from central Thailand and now studying in Bangkok, gave a challenging presentation of the vision behind forming a local church association. By the end of the meeting, the three churches had agreed in principle to form a local branch of the Associated Churches of Thailand. This was an exciting first step in building fellowship together and was formalised a year later. It would bear much fruit in years to come.

I was keen to see more churches planted in Bangkok. Sadly, the Area Council, which decided where new OMF workers were sent, appeared to have little vision for church planting in the capital, and mostly sent new arrivals elsewhere. Jenny and I began to wonder, therefore, whether we could do some church planting ourselves. If we gave responsibility for Study House to another couple, we could move the office to a crowded residential area and start a church there.

We began to pray for three things: a suitable couple to run Study House, guidance to a new location for ourselves and the office, and more people to join the church-planting team.

The answers began to come. By mid-1988 Dave and Jan Rika, serving in the south of Thailand, were looking for a new role and agreed to take over running the Study House.

As for an outreach location, early in 1988 as I was driving home from a church service, I accidentally found myself in the winding streets of a district called Huai Khwang, with its high-rise flats, cramped townhouses, and open markets. 'A perfect place for church planting,' I thought as I headed through the area.

Now we began to focus on where we would live in Huai Khwang. To our amazement the first place we looked at seemed just right, and the owner was preparing a move himself. As there were no other housing offers made to us, we agreed to rent the property.

We moved in November 1988. A challenge now presented itself – the building had previously housed a large number of idols. So our first step, as in all new houses we rented, was to walk through the building, praying for the Lord's cleansing, protection, and peace. There was an extra dimension too. The 'resident spirit' occupying the 'spirit house' in the garden was being worshipped by our landlord. Therefore, following his monthly visits, its influence needed to be neutralised by our prayer of faith, so peace and joy was maintained.

The new set-up ran well. Team fellowship was deepening at the monthly prayer meetings that were continuing at the Study House. That place was thriving under the Rikas' management. Meanwhile we were freed up both to visit team members and to do some local church planting. We continued to pray for new teammates to join us in the church-planting ministry.

We were all set for fruitful ministry. Or so we thought.

13

ALL THINGS FOR GOOD

The year 1989 began on a positive note with a special meeting between four churches in Bangkok forming the Bangkok branch of the Associated Churches of Thailand. The three churches that had met on the *Logos* the previous year had been joined by another one, recently started by new OMF workers. This grouping strengthened the links between churches and gave new vision to church planting in the city. I invited the leaders to have a quarterly meeting at our house, with their wives meeting together with Jenny at the same time. These sessions were greatly appreciated, and were soon held in the different churches in turn.

The church leaders now began to think of the future and whether more churches could be planted in Bangkok. A faith-plan was adopted, aiming to start six new churches in the next six years!

The first new church was the one we helped start in Huai Khwang. Here Jenny and I had been spending one day a week in the community, making friends, and selling Christian literature from the book trolley we had previously used in Tha Tako. The OMF publishers had just moved their premises into Huai Khwang and had a meeting room available where the new group could be started. A year later this growing church had purchased an old house in the area to use for its meetings. Now five churches were left to plant!

We were delighted to see the Bangkok team's growth in unity and purpose, and especially its growing concern for church planting. But as we began to prepare for home assignment at the end of 1989, it looked like this work was about to be undone.

Proposed changes in the structure of OMF Thailand meant the members of the Bangkok team we had worked so hard to build would be divided up. Instead there would be teams based on the different ministries across the country. Our leadership position would disappear, and the newly opened office and ministry centre in Huai Khwang would be closed down. I was particularly sad that the momentum in church planting in Bangkok would be lost.

Despite my concerns, and those my some of my colleagues, the new policy was implemented. Before long the Bangkok team was dissolved, with consequent loss of cohesion and direction. It would be several years before the damage caused would be recognised, the policy reversed, and a Bangkok team formed again.

How would we and our fellow team members, some of whom were upset, cope with the proposals? Could we continue to work with colleagues who had refused to listen to our concerns? The answer given to me by the Lord was to deliberately forgive them in my heart and to pray for God's blessing on their lives and ministries. As such, any root of bitterness was removed, and I could continue serving with them in good fellowship in the future.

After a 10-month home assignment, we returned to Thailand in late 1990. Romans 8:28 promises 'that in all things God works for the good of those who love him'. We began to see this fulfilled in our ministry in Bangkok. No longer being in leadership gave Jenny and me more time for 'hands-on' ministry in Bangkok with the five churches we had been working with before. As well as helping them plant five more churches, we introduced the Home Bible Seminary programme we had used successfully in Tha Tako.

This was a great opportunity, in small groups, to cover the whole Bible in five years, with fortnightly studies and homework in between. How special to have on one side of the table the highly educated boss of a government department and on the other side a coarse-speaking noodle seller, both united in their desire to know God's word better and serve him more effectively. Despite widely differing education levels, the groups stuck together and grew in spiritual maturity through their times together.

Meanwhile Jenny helped in evangelistic classes teaching English. Her training as a speech therapist brought an invitation to help children with speech difficulties at the Pak Kret orphanage for disabled children, run by Christian Outreach. She also helped two days a week at the Baan Nokkamin home for boys, which was started by a Swiss OMF worker, Erwin Groebli, and led to another church being planted.

I had now been appointed coordinator of the OMF church-planting team in Bangkok, which had grown to 14 members, working alongside 15 full-time Thai church workers. It was a great joy to join the six Bangkok churches – numbering 150 adults and 50 children – for their first joint camp at the seaside in August 1991. Seventeen believers were baptised in the sea, eight professed Christ publicly, and 17 consecrated their lives for full-time service. Fellowship days and camps became a regular and important part of church life.

As it happened, our faith-goal of six new churches by 1995 would be exceeded! Altogether nine churches were now in place, together with two new church-planting initiatives. Today there are over 30 churches in the Associated Churches of Thailand Bangkok group. God graciously gave us the privilege of being part of their story.

14

HOME CALL

Even though I walk through the darkest valley ...
you are with me (Psalm 23:4).

Towards the end of August 1993 Jenny had begun to experience severe back pain, and normal painkillers had no effect. So she went to the OMF hospital at Manorom for an examination. With the doctors unable to reach a clear diagnosis, exploratory surgery was proposed. This was carried out on 22 September by two surgeons, with the operation lasting several hours. They discovered and removed a tumour, about the size of an orange, which was attached to the inside of Jenny's spine.

When the surgeons shared with me what they had found, I was shocked by this discovery. It was something that even these experienced medics had never seen before. They indicated that Jenny's condition was very serious and probably a malignant form of cancer, which was later confirmed. This deeply disappointing outcome hit hard. But at the same time, Jenny and I sensed that the Lord knew all about her disease and would bring us through. His promise that 'I am with you always' (Matthew 28:20) was still true. As Jenny and I digested the news, we resolved together to focus on her best care and quality of life, whatever the outcome.

After her operation Jenny spent several more weeks at Manorom, hoping to regain strength and mobility. A constant flow of visitors from Tha Tako, Pai Sali, and elsewhere uplifted us by their loving presence and earnest and heartfelt prayers.

Sadly Jenny's condition failed to improve, and plans were put in place to evacuate her to the UK for further treatment. Her damaged spine meant she could no longer walk, so an improvised 'ambulance' served to move her to the mission home in Bangkok. Here again the love of the Bangkok team members and Thai believers touched our hearts. The cost to have Jenny flown back to England was very high as she would need the space of six plane seats. Wonderfully this was covered by donations given by Thai believers.

Jenny and I flew back on 27 October, and she was directly transferred to the Christie Hospital in Manchester, which specialises in cancer care. She stayed there for two weeks. Even though Jenny received the best possible treatment, it was not successful.

During her stay at Christie's, our church leaders came to pray with her, anointing her with oil in the Lord's name. A miracle of sorts took place at that point. Though not physically healed, Jenny no longer feared death and instead experienced the Lord's deep peace.

Subsequently Jenny was transferred to a hospice not far from our family home in north Manchester. In my daily visits, we shared precious thoughts from the Bible and prayed, but didn't talk about her dying – I don't think either of us could speak of that.

But she did occasionally ask me, 'How long do I have to live?'

'I don't know,' I would reply. 'Only that your life will be shortened. And in the meantime we will make it as special as possible.'

Her two-month stay in the hospice was a very precious time for us as a family. Jenny took every opportunity to comfort fellow patients in the Lord's name, praying with them and for them. The diaries she kept at that time are filled with words of thanksgiving and praise to the Lord. Each day she would observe something precious – two squirrels playing on the lawn outside, an unexpected letter and gift from Thailand, visits by family and friends – all giving joy and gratitude.

Hannah and Paul were each living in different parts of the UK. But miraculously, on the eve of 15 January 1994, both had a strong compulsion to return to Jenny's bedside immediately, Paul travelling through the night to be there. The following morning, just one hour after they arrived, Jenny went peacefully to be with the Lord, with me and the children singing songs of Zion to help her on the way.

We three wept, hugged, and prayed together, thanking God for her wonderful life. We could hardly believe she had gone, but were comforted to know that she had entered the glorious presence of the Lord, who she loved and served.

After a while we went home and began to think of the future. Hannah and Paul looked after me wonderfully and made sure all was in place for the funeral, to be held in a week's time. After that I said farewell to them as they returned to their different parts of the country, and then headed into the future by myself, but with the Lord ever by my side.

15

PRESSING ON

'Dearly loved wife, mother, and missionary to Thailand.' So read the words engraved in gold letters on Jenny's gravestone. Then underneath, in both English and Thai, was a quotation: 'For me to live is Christ' (cf. Philippians 1:21). Such was her life and service for God.

The cemetery where Jenny was buried was not far from our family home in Manchester, and it became a precious place for me during the first year after she died. The pain of separation was more severe than I expected. It would take a full year for the 'inner ice' of mourning to melt and my emotions to become more normal again. Once a week I would take some flowers from our garden, together with some of Jenny's letters, and spend time at the graveside. There I would read the letters, shed tears of grief, and then pray.

After the many wonderful expressions of love and sympathy had ended, and the caring community of friends, relatives, and church family had moved on,

I began to feel the keen loneliness of my new situation. Hannah's and Paul's regular visits were a great comfort and blessing. At the same time I brought my strongly felt need for a new life companion to the Lord in prayer, and tried to leave it there!

Meanwhile I was regularly attending our local Independent Methodist church, where Jenny and I had been members for many years. One Sunday morning, just a month after the funeral, I was walking home from the church and pondering whether my missionary career had finished. I recalled the passage that had been expounded at the service – the incident of the burning bush in Exodus 3. Then Moses resisted God's call, giving every possible reason why he should not return to Egypt and bring God's people out from there.

This was the same passage that God had used to call me to missionary service 30 years earlier. At that time I too had raised every possible reason for resisting God's call, until every one was answered by God's assurance: 'That's not your problem, that's my problem!' Likewise this Sunday morning God heard all my concerns as to why I should not continue in missionary service. Again he met them with his assurance that they all were his responsibility. So before reaching home I prayed, recommitting myself to return to overseas missionary service.

In consultation with the OMF leadership, my year's home assignment in the UK was extended to two years with a one-year MA course at London Bible College, starting in September 1994.

The prospect of a 'quietish' six months before starting my MA was very attractive. Imagine my indignation therefore when OMF proposed that I go to Bristol for five months to cover the West Regional Director position, prior to someone else taking over long-term!

Misgivings aside, I went and found it, in fact, a very helpful time. I was serving among people who hadn't known Jenny or our family situation, so I was back in a socially 'normal' environment. There were challenges too, not least running two homes (in Bristol from Monday to Friday, and in Manchester for the weekends) and two cars (one belonging to OMF, the other my own), as well as learning a new job from scratch.

Getting to know a new part of the country was quite special, and it was encouraging to see something of the support for global mission throughout the region. I was responsible for the care of OMF workers on home assignment, dealing with enquiries about serving God overseas, and connecting with supporters and prayer partners throughout the area.

One special touch of the Lord's care for me at this time stands out. For 18 months my Manchester house would be empty on weekdays. Who would look after it when I wasn't there? It was my practice each evening to pray that the Lord, through his holy angels, would keep the property safe. At the end of my time away I discovered that every other house in my road had been burgled except mine!

Before starting at London Bible College, I needed to renew my Thai visa. When I first went to Thailand, I was fortunate to be issued a 'permanent' visa, which was very precious as these soon stopped being issued. However, one of its conditions was that the visa holder couldn't be out of the country for longer than a year. So I made a week-long visit to Thailand to renew my visa. I had a very warm welcome from the team there, themselves still coming to terms with Jenny's death.

As for myself, though I continued to mourn Jenny's passing, I also had peace in my mind about her. I had come to realise that her life in God's eyes was complete and beautiful and didn't need any additions. It was like a painting, now finished and needing signing off. So before God I deliberately released her to his care – I was now no longer responsible for her.

This 'peaceful mindset' was helpful when sharing fellowship with missionary colleagues in Bangkok. Several of them urged me to remarry, and one even prayed openly in a team meeting for a suitable new wife for me! I also had time to talk about a future church-planting strategy with team members. Two families who were looking to plant a church on the west bank of the Chao Phraya River in Bangkok invited me to join their team when I returned to Thailand next year.

My time at Bible college – studying the Old Testament, the Holy Spirit, and hermeneutics – was more difficult than I expected. The first two subjects were accessible, but the third was almost beyond my reach. I worked hard to cover the large amount of material presented. Though I certainly did not master it all, by the end I felt I had gained sufficient understanding to teach the Bible more effectively.

The group on the MA course became a happy, close unit, and we were able to encourage one another as we faced difficulties in our studies. Many years later I am still in prayer fellowship with several of them.

On the social side, it was not easy being in the presence of about 300 single lady students, most of whom were bright, godly, and attractive. My felt need for a life partner was ever present, and I was forever going back to God in prayer for his guidance in this area. I knew that the right person must have a clear missionary call and the capability to serve alongside me in the challenges of missionary life in East Asia. One potential person ruled themselves out immediately by announcing they didn't like curries – a staple of most Thai meals! In the end, despite some slightly more promising possibilities, no one emerged as right for me. I wondered if the Lord would have someone for me when I returned to Asia.

While at college I attended the regular mission prayer meetings for East Asia. On one occasion, in February 1995, we were praying for Cambodia. The situation there sounded grim, with the country suffering deeply in the aftermath of the Khmer Rouge years and the subsequent civil war. We also heard about the severe restrictions on foreigners being in the country. I came away feeling sorry for anyone called to serve there.

The next day I returned early to Manchester as I was not feeling well. Looking through the letters waiting for me, I saw one with a Thailand stamp. It was from Ian Roberts, a senior OMF Director. He began by explaining there were currently seven OMF workers serving in Cambodia but no team leader to help them expand their ministry there. Would I be willing to take on that role when my home assignment in the UK ended later in the year?

I must confess I laughed at the Lord for this extraordinary timing. Then I knelt and prayed, asking him if this was his will for me. The immediate conviction given by the Holy Spirit was 'yes, this is my will for you'. A minute later I stood up, knowing this invitation was his next step for me. I also talked to Hannah, Paul, and ministry colleagues, who were universally supportive. Even the team I was due to serve with in Bangkok agreed with the change. The general feeling seemed to be that a new challenge was what I needed and it was time for me to move forward. With this support behind me, I wrote a letter of acceptance.

At Easter 1995 I had to return to Thailand to again renew my visa. I got an update from Ian Roberts and a welcome message from the team I would be leading in Cambodia. I was also given two cassette tapes of the

Cambodian language, with the hope I could learn some of it before I got there!

After completing my MA and a moving farewell service at my church, in November 1995 I arrived in Bangkok and then took a connecting flight in a small aircraft to Phnom Penh, the capital of Cambodia. A wave of fears swept in. What would it be like to work in a new country I had never visited and whose language I couldn't speak? Would there be anyone to meet me as I arrived in a strange country? As we came into land, I was reminded of the leading and faithfulness of the Lord, and committed myself to trust him.

The arrivals hall in the small airport was a sea of people jostling in all directions, watched over by heavily armed guards. There was nobody I could recognise. Then I saw an arm waving in the distance, belonging to the friendly face of Ajarn Narin, one of my old colleagues from Thailand.

I had arrived and was not alone: a new adventure awaited.

PART TWO

BULLETS

CAMBODIA

16

NEW COUNTRY, NEW CHALLENGES

I woke at 2 a.m. to the sound of machine gunfire.

Tat-tat-tat-tat.

Tat-tat-tat – more machine gunfire rattled from further away.

My worst fears surfaced. It must be the Khmer Rouge staging a comeback, I reasoned, and I am in the middle of it! I knew they were still active in the northwest of the country, but surely not here in Phnom Penh, the capital of Cambodia?

I crawled to the window and peeped out, but there was nothing much to see. So I went back to bed, though still very apprehensive.

I had been in Cambodia just a few days, and was staying temporarily at the home of Thai friends Narin and his wife, Wilairat. They had been serving as OMF missionaries in Cambodia a couple of years already, and were involved in a church plant near Phnom Penh airport.

The next morning my first question was, 'What was that?'

'Oh, nothing to worry about!' they said. 'There was a fire in one of the nearby houses, and people fired their guns in the air to alert the neighbourhood, so people could come and help put it out.'

It was a dramatic introduction to the challenges facing Cambodia. It lacked regular services such as a functioning fire brigade. Yet most people still had their own guns after the four years of the Khmer Rouge 'killing fields' (1975–1979) and the subsequent occupation of the country by the Vietnamese, which had only ended in 1989. Lawlessness was widespread and vigilante groups of 'irregular' soldiers set up roadblocks at will, ready to extract 'protection' money from road users.

The war damage was striking as I explored the city. The roads still had massive potholes, many now sprouting grass. These were overlooked by ruined houses, while those buildings still standing looked grimy – it seemed nothing had been painted for many years. There were few cars on the roads. Those that could be seen were mostly a dirty white, being the vehicles left behind by the UN peace-keeping force when they withdrew three years earlier. Most people got around on small motorbikes that seemed to carry as many passengers as were able to squeeze on.

I soon acquired a second-hand motorbike, though not for long. Within a week it had been stolen. I reflected that while it had taken seven years for my first motorbike in

Thailand to be stolen, here it had only taken seven days! It underlined both the severe poverty of the Cambodian people and the need to take care of one's property.

However, not everything was gloomy to look at. Bicycle pedicabs with their elegant hoods still roamed the streets, a reminder of the days when Cambodia was a French colony. The French influence also showed itself in the wide-brimmed straw hats favoured by the women, the stacks of baguette-style bread on stalls along the roadside, and a 'Gendarmerie' sign over the police station door.

The OMF team in Cambodia now had ten members. Most of these were quite new and still in Phnom Penh doing language study, though Rosa Brand and Alice Compain were veterans of previous ministry in Cambodia and with Cambodian refugees. It was daunting to lead a team where everyone had more experience here than I had. I would have to trust the Lord to help me, especially in these early days of building a team. I took comfort from the promise of Proverbs 16:3, 'Commit to the Lord whatever you do, and he will establish your plans.'

One of my first tasks as team leader was to find suitable premises to use for a team centre. So Rosa, Alice, and I scoured the city, and found somewhere suitable in the Tuol Kork area near central Phnom Penh. The rent requested was far too high, but my bargaining skills learned in Thailand eventually helped secure a good price.

The place needed to be thoroughly cleaned and refurbished, a responsibility that also fell on me. So with nine bedrooms to choose from, I changed my room every night, using the previous day to make it useable. Soon there were spaces for my office, a meeting room, and a dining room.

Now I was set up with a desk and a phone, I could begin to face the floods of correspondence that were arriving every day. But with my minimal knowledge of the country, its church, and OMF internationally, prayer was crucial. As each unanswerable letter came in, I would kneel on the floor of the office, asking the Lord what to say. Without exception he would give me the answer, I would send it off, and then I would proceed to the next letter.

Another challenge was getting money for the team members. A US dollar was valued at 3000 riel, the Cambodian currency. So small items were paid for with riel, and larger ones with dollars. And because the riel came in stacks of grubby banknotes, you needed a large purse to care for the bundles provided. Most streets had money changers who were happy to help!

Our bank was on the other side of the city, so once a month I cycled there and collected several thousand dollars in cash that team members needed to pay their expenses. Then with a shoulder bag full of banknotes, I would cycle vigorously back across the city, hoping I was not being pursued! It was only several years later that we moved to a less traumatic means of money transfer.

Alongside all this, I had to learn the Cambodian language,

which I found much harder than I expected. Even though a third of the words had a similar spelling to Thai, the pronunciation was quite different. I realised that in reality I had to start from scratch. For three months I did a language course at Phnom Penh University, but sadly made little progress. A different approach was needed. So for the next few years, I hired a retired Cambodian soldier to come to the team centre every day to teach me. We spent 30 minutes early in the morning practising reading and conversation. Gradually I acquired enough language for basic conversation and to preach in local churches.

Although on a practical level OMF was on its way to becoming established in Cambodia, I was aware of a problem. Even though we were a small team of 10 who mostly lived in the same city, I found that the members were so focused on their individual ministries that they almost seemed unwilling to spend time together as a group. Though Christmas was coming, there was little interest in doing anything together. But, to my mind, if we were going to be an effective working team, it was essential we spent time together to get to know each other.

Undaunted, on 23 December 1995 I told them that if they would like to join me in celebrating Christmas Day, they would be welcome. 'If you come,' I added, 'bring a food dish and some family photos.' The next day I made a Christmas 'tree' out of some cardboard boxes and decorated it. Wonderfully, on Christmas Day they all came, and we had an excellent time of worship, games, and looking at family photos together. A first step in growing team fellowship had taken place.

Building on this, I stressed that in Christ we should care for one another and that sharing time together was important to build a strong team. I introduced occasional 'team picnics', when we would hire a bus – or, on one memorable occasion, a boat – to go off to a place of interest for the day. Not only did we get to see some ancient temples and beautiful scenery, but we were able to get to know each other better. We began a weekly team prayer meeting that fostered a real sense of fellowship. In addition, team members serving outside Phnom Penh were always included in our prayers.

Our registration with the government allowed us to do evangelism and church planting, provided we did an equal amount of development work. The latter was going well in our teaching work at schools and universities, with a wide range of care services to follow. But what about starting new churches, our essential purpose for being in Cambodia? How could I help lead in this area?

During the Khmer Rouge period, the national church had been decimated, with only 1000 believers surviving. But since then the church had started to grow again. By 1995 it had reached 18,000 believers in 200 churches.

This made the Cambodian church one of the fastest growing in the world at the time. One reason was that during the communist period, the national Buddhist religion had largely been dismantled, leaving a spiritual vacuum. Another was the burden of guilt and shame that many people still experienced from the Khmer Rouge time. In the church they found a place of forgiveness and acceptance, and a new start.

It seemed that this was God's time for Cambodia. Much prayer and faith had been extended towards this suffering land. People now seemed open to the concept of a living God in whom was the love and forgiveness for which they longed.

How then was our OMF team to contribute to the growth of the church? Even before I arrived in Cambodia, the Lord had given me a set of possible goals to use for the OMF team. These were that we would plant three churches in Phnom Penh and three outside the capital.

On my arrival in Cambodia, I found that there was already one OMF church plant in Phnom Penh, supported by my Thai friends Narin and Wilairat. And in the county town of Kratie, a six-hour boat ride to the north up the Mekong River, the Cooper family from the UK were doing initial outreach. I was encouraged by this good start but wanted the team to think where else we could start new churches.

I knew that effective church planting required understanding the Cambodian people better. It was clear that their need was inner peace. One taxi driver told me that of his 23 relatives, he was the only survivor from the Khmer Rouge killing fields. Like him, many were still trying to recover from the trauma of 20 years earlier. Others shared how their spouses had been taken away or been killed in front of them. One lady said she herself had been taken away, along with other villagers, to be killed. They were lined up in front of a trench that was to take their bodies. Then, at the last moment, the Vietnamese military advance reached the village, and their captors fled.

It was incredibly hard to know how to help such people. But it seemed that simply sharing their story, perhaps many times, was therapeutic for them. I spent many hours just listening and hopefully bringing some word of encouragement. If they were open to it, I would share that God himself, in his Son, had suffered severely like them. He had even asked that the perpetrators be forgiven. Maybe they could move towards forgiveness, the only cure for a damaged heart.

I would also occasionally reflect myself on the extent of the suffering that had taken place and why God had allowed it. Certainly the extreme wickedness shown had come direct from the evil one and all his forces of evil, as listed in Ephesians 6:12. However, the result was that there was now surprising openness to the good news about Jesus. People in their thousands were getting opportunities to hear and respond to the gospel message.

17

RELATIONSHIPS

The 10 members when I arrived in late 1995 had grown to 17 missionaries by June 1996. The new arrivals were not only from Europe and North America, but were also from across Southeast Asia. Eventually half of our team members were of Asian origin.

The different perspectives brought by our Asian colleagues were a great stimulus to the team. Their unashamed zeal for gospel proclamation and church planting meant they were often at the forefront of new outreach initiatives. They brought much-needed encouragement to those of us from a more 'reserved' Western background.

However, communications across the team weren't always straightforward. Team meetings, which covered issues from the trivial – 'Where should we go for our next team outing?' – to the more serious – 'What is an appropriate level of pastoral care for each family?' – would be dominated by us Westerners, who had been taught to 'speak our minds'. They were happy to disagree, if necessary, with what I had proposed. In contrast, my Asian colleagues would mostly keep quiet so I didn't lose face or be 'shamed' through public disagreement. Somehow I needed their opinion too. One approach was to break up into small groups to discuss the question. When I then asked for feedback from each group, we heard from all sides.

Often, though, the true thoughts of the Asian team members were conveyed to me after the meeting had concluded. For example, an invitation to a meal might arrive, providing the opportunity to get their more 'Asian' perspective. This was so helpful in finding the best solution for each issue and working together in harmony.

I was also aware that, as the team grew, the fact that I, the team leader, was single was not straightforward neither for me nor for team members. This was especially so since the women outnumbered the men two to one and many of them were single. Having already looked in vain for a possible marriage partner at Bible college, I wondered if I might find someone among my missionary colleagues. I regularly prayed about this too. My desire was someone who could serve the Lord together with me in Cambodia, and ideally someone from the north of England – my background culture! However, normal friendships with the single women in the OMF team were surprisingly difficult. Some kept me at 'arm's length', while others came 'too close'. Despite my prayer for a suitable marriage partner and my strongly felt need, the way appeared to be closed. So, in mid-March 1996, I again approached the Lord on the matter, but this time asked that I would be content in my present situation of being single.

Before the month was over, however, there was an unexpected answer to my prayer! An OMF doctor, Rachel Hillier, who was normally based in Thailand, had come over to Cambodia for a week to carry out our team medical examinations. On one occasion she asked me if there was anything specific I would like her to pray for, so I shared my prayer about my singleness.

Two days later Dr Rachel shared that, as she prayed for me, the Lord had laid on her heart one woman: Miss Mary Gascoigne. Mary was currently working as a physiotherapist and evangelist at the OMF hospital in Sai Buri, south Thailand, so was used to missionary work in Southeast Asia. She was also from the north of England! Rachel had recently met Mary while doing medicals there and felt that Mary was looking for a new way forward in her own life, especially as the OMF hospital in south Thailand was closing.

I began to wonder if God was answering my prayer in a way I had not expected!

Rachel's suggestion was a happy surprise as Jenny and I had briefly overlapped with Mary at the new Study House in Bangkok. Mary had also got to know our daughter, Hannah, when she was a toddler. In later years Jenny and I had occasionally been in touch with Mary, and had admired her life and ministry in south Thailand. Even so, I somehow felt that Mary was 'out of reach' for a fellow like me! Competent, attractive, and self-assured, I was sure she must have her own life plans.

Nevertheless, Rachel encouraged me to make a move! So it was agreed that she would act as 'matchmaker' (since we were in Asia, and this is how they did things) and would approach Mary on my behalf. In particular she would ask Mary whether she was willing to have a special friendship with me, with a view to exploring the possibility of marriage.

Three weeks later, on 19 April, and after Rachel had returned to Thailand, I received a message saying, 'It's on!'

Eventually Mary and I got in touch by phone. Letters and phone calls then went back and forth the 500 miles between our two countries. We soon realised that we had much in common. Daily phone calls became special, but with calls costing $2 a minute from Thailand, and double the cost from Cambodia, bills mounted rapidly. In the end Mary had to sell her motorbike to pay for her calls! Letters were cheaper, but their delivery was haphazard. Sometimes three would arrive at once, leaving a dilemma as to how quickly to read them. I tried to ration them, but ended up reading all at once!

A month later, in May 1996, we had the opportunity to meet! I was due to attend a regional council meeting in Bangkok for the various ministry fields in the Mekong area. I could add on an extra day afterwards to see Mary before returning to Cambodia.

She was able to make the long overnight train journey from south Thailand to arrive that day.

We had a wonderful day together, in particular having time to share our lives' values and see what the future might hold. Returning to the mission home where we were staying, I was encouraged that we seemed to have a shared vision, but was Mary the right one for me?

We were to meet up again in about one hour. During that time, I took the opportunity to reread the passage in Proverbs 31 about the 'noble wife'. All that I knew about Mary was confirmed in these verses. I was assured that she was God's choice of partner for me. When we met again a little later, I proposed, and to my delight, she accepted.

It had all happened in one day! Early the next morning we were making our separate ways again, she to south Thailand and me back to Cambodia.

The speed of everything had taken both of us by surprise. Yet there was such a sense that this was the Lord's provision for us that we were totally at peace and full of thanksgiving at his leading. Family reaction in the UK was very positive, with both our elderly mums delighted at the news. Hannah and Paul were likewise so glad for us both. For them, of course, it would bring a new situation in their lives, which would have to be worked out in the days ahead.

Three days later I shared the news of our engagement with the OMF Cambodia team. There was a roar of acclamation from the members – a lovely assurance that we had done the right thing.

It was decided our wedding would be in the UK. But how to prepare at such a distance? In July Mary headed back to the UK to begin making initial arrangements. The wedding date was set for 2 November at her church in Newcastle.

The church members were amazingly caring and provided a wedding breakfast for 100 guests in the church hall, plus a beautiful three-tiered wedding cake. The wedding itself was unique in many ways. My son, Paul, was my best man and provided needed moral support! My daughter, Hannah, was chief bridesmaid and took time to pray with Mary before they set off for the church. The service and reception gave glory to God, and left a very favourable impression on friends and relatives still looking for life's certainties.

After an eventful honeymoon in the Lake District (where we were nearly blown off one of the higher fells!), we were soon on our way back to Cambodia in time for Christmas. There the top tier of our wedding cake provided Christmas cake for the team! Prior to going to England for the wedding, I had rented a house in Phnom Penh for us, a 10-minute bike ride from the mission home. Living in the same compound as a Cambodian family was a great learning experience for us both and provided a safety net from any harm that might come our way. Mary quickly got to know both the team and also, through her almost daily trips to the market, the local tradespeople. From Mary's perspective, moving to Cambodia wasn't the easiest transition. She had been living in a very rural situation in south Thailand, where she spoke the language well and had close relationships with the people. Now she was living in a city and couldn't speak Khmer. In addition she had to communicate more with Westerners, and tune in to their needs and aspirations. She also had to move from having an independent ministry to suddenly having a complementary role to someone in a leadership position. For example, if she was at a prayer meeting on her own, she would be invited to lead and pray. But if I was also present, people would normally ask me instead. This was just one of many challenges to work through together. Nevertheless, it helped us both that the sense of God's call to this new role and ministry was very real.

From my perspective, it was thrilling to see how God had prepared Mary for the ministry she now had in Cambodia. As 'team mother', and with her experience, energy, and gifts, she would be a great blessing to the many missionaries who would join us in Cambodia in the coming days.

18

LEADING THE TEAM

Mr Sophea, my Cambodian secretary, and I stood on the pavement outside the Ministry of Religion, wondering what to do. A keen Christian young man, Mr Sophea had now been working with me in the office for a year, and was committed to seeing the work of God go forward in his country. But for the OMF team to stay in Cambodia, we needed approval from the government, and today was yet another unsuccessful visit to a government department.

The Ministry of Foreign Affairs said they needed an authorisation letter from the Ministry of Religion in order to allow the OMF team to work in Cambodia. However, the Ministry of Religion had just told us they would first need a letter from the Ministry of Foreign Affairs before they could give permission! Neither ministry would budge. Deadlock prevailed as the clock was ticking down on the date our visas expired. If we could not break this deadlock, we would have to leave the country.

We stood and prayed near the gates of the Ministry of Religion site. As we then opened our eyes, a young official passing by stopped and asked us what was the matter. We explained our dilemma, saying we didn't know what to do. He seemed sympathetic, saying he recognised me as he had heard me speaking at a Christmas event in the city.

'I work at the Ministry of Religion,' he told us. 'I'll see what I can do. Come and see me here tomorrow.' We returned the following day, and to our great joy our papers had been signed. The whole process of renewing our visas could now proceed. It was a real answer to prayer!

Nevertheless, the next step – getting sponsorship from eight government ministries for our development team to present to the Ministry of Foreign Affairs – was a lengthy process. Facing this administration overload, again we looked to the Lord for help. It then happened that a Christian lady from the Ministry of Agriculture called to see us on a business matter, and we shared our present need with her. She said she was willing to help us, and from then on joined our OMF staff and was a wonderful guide through endless government requirements for many years to come.

A new opportunity for government sponsorship now appeared. A Christian in the Ministry of Public Works told us they were looking for English teachers for their staff. Were we interested? Mary agreed to go, but never imagined that on her first day she would be faced with a class of 125 students! Despite only having done a one-week TEFL (Teaching English as a Foreign Language) training course, Mary survived the challenge. With the help of another missionary, and the use of language aptitude tests, she was able to reduce the student numbers to 2 classes of 30 in each. She then commenced an English programme, which lasted for several years. A bonus was that one of her students became her Cambodian language teacher and a good friend. This lady eventually made a quiet commitment of faith in Christ.

Mary's medical background was invaluable in helping us care for the health of team members. She was able to find safe healthcare services at a time when facilities in Cambodia were very basic. Sometimes she had to rescue team members from clinics that were going to do them more harm than good. Eventually we sent all serious cases to Thailand.

One of our basic tasks was to find suitable accommodation for new workers, and we would wander through city streets looking for places to rent. Mostly we were successful, but we did once make the mistake of establishing a family next door to an upmarket brothel!

Before long I got to know the best secondhand furniture stores in the city and became an expert in finding secondhand fridges. Decent mattresses were hard to find, but eventually I located a helpful store. One day, when I was returning to the team centre with a new double mattress on the roof of our minibus, the vehicle suddenly felt much lighter. My choice mattress was sitting in the middle of the road! With the boldness of Elijah I stopped the traffic with the bus, hauled the mattress back on the roof, and set off again with applause from the bystanders!

Caring for new team members sometimes led to other unexpected challenges. Tim and Jenny Kangas were new workers living about a mile from the team centre. One evening they invited short-term workers Colin and Gwynneth Squires from New Zealand round for dinner. The Squireses had taken early retirement and had come to help with music ministry and English teaching. As Mary and I were closing up the team centre for the night, Mary took a phone call from Jenny. 'You're not going to believe this,' Jenny said, 'Colin Squires has just died.'

It appeared that while the others were chatting, Colin had gone to rest on the sofa. Sometime later, as everyone returned to the lounge and spoke to Colin, they found him dead.

'We'll be right there, don't do anything,' Mary told Jenny. She hurried over by motorbike while I tried to contact key people in OMF by phone. But no one was accepting calls that night – I got everyone's answerphone. I only managed to tell the OMF office in New Zealand what had happened.

I jumped in the OMF minibus and set off after Mary, but I was almost not quick enough. A friendly neighbour had already called an ambulance, and Colin's body was being taken off somewhere. With private ambulance companies and multiple hospitals in the area, his body could have been going anywhere! We followed in hot pursuit, and eventually caught up at a local hospital, just before the body was admitted to the morgue. Arranging a post-mortem, a death certificate in two languages, and later export documentation to return the ashes to New Zealand was almost an experience too far!

The funeral was held in one of the city churches, and it was very moving to welcome a large contingent from the Ministry of Public Works, where Colin had been teaching English. Many had never been in a Christian church before. We appreciated the care of Cambodian Christian friends who made arrangements for the cremation.

In this major crisis, God was with us in every practical detail. Colin's widow, Gwynneth, was greatly upheld by the Lord and his people, to the extent that she later returned for further service in Cambodia.

Our team were now being well cared for. They were learning the language and culture, and moving towards active ministry. My priority for the team was to see Cambodian people come to faith and form local churches. I wanted us to work in harmony with other churches and groups as much as possible, so whenever I could I visited and preached at local Cambodian churches.

My preaching initially was done by translation, but I discovered that the translators' English was not much better than my Cambodian. So I switched to using Khmer

(Cambodian) and everyone seemed happier. Even when I mixed in some Thai, nobody seemed to mind!

A precious opportunity for co-working with local churches came at Christmas 1997, with a two-day inter-church festival at the 5000-seat Olympic stadium. (Despite its name, the stadium has never hosted the Olympics!) There were to be three preaching sessions each day, with mine to be the last on Christmas Day. Despite severe back pain on the day, I made it on to the platform, and remarkably the pain then lifted. The Lord used my simple message on the three wise men, given by translation, to touch many hearts. We heard later that from the huge crowd 560 decisions for Christ had been recorded.

I continued to encourage team members either to work with our existing church plants or to start new ones. The work of my Thai friends Narin and Wilairat in Pochentong district of Phnom Penh had a good start, but faded when they went on home assignment. On their return they introduced a new cell-church set-up, ensuring every member was discipled and cared for, and the church then experienced solid growth. Eventually the group moved out of the mission home and relocated in a large derelict house they had purchased. The building was in use every day, the fellowship of believers being a vital part of church life. Recognising that some of the members had a real love for God's word, Narin gave them extra Bible teaching on a regular basis, and one of them eventually became a pastor.

We also emphasised the importance of church planting outside the capital. As well as occasionally visiting the existing church plant in Kratie, six hours away, we surveyed other parts of the country where we might start more new churches. Even though half of our team were engaged in development work, I was keen that each member was part of a church-planting team. Those touched by practical expressions of God's love should have opportunity to hear a gospel message too.

An early example of this was in the Calmette area in north Phnom Penh. Here missionaries teaching at the school of music brought together some of their students for a weekly Bible study. This group began to grow, encouraged by a Korean missionary, Chul Hun, who was a member of the church-planting team.

As the group grew, Chul Hun rented an open 'shop front' building and started Sunday worship services there. He had a burden to help male students coming to study in the city. Being an expert in taekwondo, the Korean martial art, he started classes in this for the young men, and soon had made friends with many of them.

With my encouragement he then rented separate premises to serve as a hostel for them. Over the next few months he progressively led them to faith in Christ, and then continued to disciple and train them. Before long he was taking them with him to do evangelism in neighbouring villages and was able to start church groups in several of these. Eventually seven new groups were started, and the young men who had been instrumental in this became their part-time pastors!

One day Chul Hun came to me with a new vision. 'I want to put up a large church building, seating several hundred people, close to where our Phnom Penh group is meeting. I have seen some land and can get funds from Korea to do it. What do you think?'

We looked over the large site that was up for sale, and I gave him the go ahead. Within two years a large church building, the 'Jesus village church', was in place and filled with Cambodians who had come to Christ through this Calmette ministry. It was so encouraging to be able to help my team flourish in their roles and take 'faith strides' forward.

Not all our church-planting work was successful, though. Our attempts to start a third church in Phnom Penh ran into constant problems. Over several years we tried three different initiatives in the south of the city. Each lasted about a year but in the end folded up, with the missionaries having lost heart or needing to relocate. We realised that not everyone's gifting was in church planting, and several were more fruitful doing other ministries, such as Christian publishing.

With three churches now planted by the OMF team, we began to think about linking them up together, just as Narin and I had done in Bangkok a decade earlier. So at a special meeting at the Calmette church in May 1998, the Kratie, Pochentong, and Calmette churches became founder members of Fellowship Churches of Cambodia.

This group was for OMF-planted churches and any others who wanted to join. Mr Heng Cheng, the General Secretary of Evangelical Fellowship of Cambodia, preached at the service. He shared that the Protestant church was growing at 30% a year, so that the 18,000 members in 1995 were now 40,000 in 1998.

The work nationwide was growing, and we were thrilled to be part of it. It was with much joy, despite our exhaustion, that we packed up for our next home assignment.

19

PUSHING FORWARD

Our physical and emotional recovery got underway now we were back in Manchester. The cooler weather, English food and language, and precious family times together all helped. Churches nationwide gave us a warm welcome, especially the Independent Methodists in England and those of the United Free churches in Scotland. These were the churches that had supported Mary and me – individually and now together – over many years. It was a joy to share some of what we had seen God doing in Cambodia.

Though we enjoyed this sharing ministry, with over 100 meetings before us, it was difficult to keep fresh and excited. One strategy that kept us focused was selling books on world mission at these meetings. I developed a good selling approach, which I had learned from George Verwer, the founder of Operation Mobilisation and a very enthusiastic bookseller. During the year, books worth many hundreds of pounds were purchased. This helped us gauge people's response to our message, and we trusted God would continue working through the books after we left.

By May 2001 it was time to return to Cambodia. Now fully refreshed, we were ready for the new opportunities of service ahead. Arriving back we were pleased to find we no longer needed to manage the mission home, an extra load on us in our previous missionary term. Harry and Carol Blagden from the UK had taken on that responsibility. Harry had observed that, with 50 team members and a growing need for better facilities, a purpose-built team centre was now needed. We had previously rented the mission home building, but now owned it outright so redevelopment was possible.

David Gould, an OMF colleague and an architect, provided us with plans for a three-storey facility incorporating features from traditional Cambodian buildings. In November 2001 a contract was signed with a local building firm, and the office moved temporarily down the street.

The site was cleared and building work began. One day the firm's director asked us, 'When is the ceremony?' From his religious background, no building could proceed without one. So I called the team members to the site and, with Bible readings and prayers, we consecrated the foundations and building to the glory of God. Happy that the project was now under divine care, the company got on with the job, completing the building within six months.

A large sign, 'Have faith in God' (Mark 11:22), was carved in concrete at the front, in both English and

Cambodian languages, as a testimony to all who passed by. The opening ceremony was performed in July 2002 by the OMF General Director, David Harley. Today the team centre continues to provide a refuge for team members, with facilities including accommodation, a library, language labs, dining rooms, a large meeting hall, and ample office space.

Another welcome change was an administrative one which upgraded my position as 'Superintendent' to 'Field Director'. This allowed me to share my workload by appointing three regional coordinators to oversee church planting, development work, and language and orientation respectively. We also formed local teams, with each person in a smaller team for encouragement and pastoral care.

The development work of our team ministry continued to grow. One new initiative was the provision of hostel accommodation for vulnerable factory girls who had come to work in Phnom Penh. Other centres were opened – one for former prostitutes and another for children with disabilities. A care ministry for former prisoners was also started. Up in Kratie province we ran a literacy programme for those unable to read, and in Kompong Cham we opened a hostel for AIDS sufferers. All these were areas of felt need at this point in the nation's life and provided ways to share the gospel in both word and deed.

On the church-planting front, our earlier surveys of potential church-planting locations were now bearing fruit. On one trip south of Phnom Penh, as Mary and

I crossed the Mekong River by ferry, I noticed a fair-sized town on the far shore, on the road eastwards to Vietnam. So when a new Korean missionary couple, Hak Hyun and Seung Won, were looking to start church planting, I mentioned this town of Neak Luong to them.

They were keen to start a church there, but wisely preferred to have a local Christian in their team. They spent two years learning culture and language at Narin and Wilairat's Pochentong church in Phnom Penh. A member of that church, Ms Srey Oun, then went with them to Neak Luong to begin outreach there. After five years they had planted a viable church, with its own building and local leadership.

Whatever kind of ministry team members were doing, an important part of my role was to help them fulfil their potential for God's kingdom. Writing a personal job description for each of them was a great help in achieving this, but we also had regular life and ministry reviews with each worker. As the majority of the team were women, I aimed to have Mary with me at every interview. Apart from wanting to be above reproach, I knew this would make the women feel more comfortable and more open in their responses. Deep personal issues would sometimes surface, and with the Lord's help we were able to work through most of these. Very occasionally I would encounter non-cooperation from some team members, and that I found very difficult to deal with. I felt personally sad when my attempts to seek a common way forward were unsuccessful.

A favourite part of our role were opportunities to visit colleagues and local Christians in more rural areas, reminding us both of happy years spent in different parts of rural Thailand. One visit took us to see Mr Reaksa in north Cambodia and some new churches planted there. He was the only surviving member of his family from the Khmer Rouge killing fields. His escape, journey to faith in Christ, and how he found inner healing is told in his book, *Tears of My Soul.*[1]

Travelling further westwards, we came to the village of Kompong Speu. 'We have done outreach here,' Reaksa told us, 'but though there are some believers, they refuse to meet together.'

It happened that our car broke down outside the home of a lady Reaksa knew in the village. While the car was being fixed, we chatted to her and found out she was a Christian.

'Why don't you start a Christian group?' I challenged her.

She laughed at me. 'I have no voice, and my husband is very shy,' she told me.

But our word had struck home. We later heard that, after we left, the couple felt convicted by God that they should do something. So they contacted the other believers they knew in the town. A regular meeting began

1 Sokreaksa S. Himm, *Tears of My Soul* (Lion Hudson, 2003).

from that, and it was gratifying to hear a short while later that 25 people were meeting to worship each Sunday!

Further field trips took us to Ratanakiri in the northeast, to encourage our work among the Kreung, Brao, and Tumpuan tribal people. In the south we visited a new church-planting initiative in the coastal town of Kep. And in central Cambodia we visited some Western Cham people, where team members were beginning to work.

While there were lots of opportunities, these initiatives were not always followed up. One difficulty was the reluctance of some missionary families to live in rural areas. Not only were healthcare and children's education an issue, but so was personal security. Some felt vulnerable in a land that was formerly a place of immense suffering and pain. Such fear needed to be recognised and overcome by deliberate trust in God's care.

Even in Phnom Penh, Mary and I experienced the need for the Lord's protection. For example, one evening we were returning home from the team centre by motorbike and had, to go along an unlit alleyway. About a third of the way along we saw two men moving out of the shadows, clearly armed, ready to intercept us. As we prayed quickly to the Lord for his help, suddenly a motorbike entered the alley from the opposite direction. The two men withdrew into the shadows, and we passed by unharmed. 'Has God sent his angel to help us?' we wondered with thanksgiving.

Dealing with fears and apprehensions was important for each team member. At the same time we recognised the sacrifice many made as they willingly moved out of their comfort zone.

In all this it gave us great joy to see the growing faith of the Cambodian believers and their desire to share the gospel with others. Christmas celebrations in the churches were a great opportunity to share the gospel, and even the smallest churches would attract lots of visitors.

In Neak Luong, where Hak Hyun and Seung Won were working, the church invited friends and neighbours to a Christmas celebration in 2003. Over 200 attended, including some local government officials. Our role in all these occasions was to provide encouragement, especially in the area of intentional follow-up with those who showed interest.

The Fellowship Churches of Cambodia now had its own committee, which was vital for the future growth and direction of this group of churches. They began by organising a conference for existing and potential church leaders, and 55 people attended. In 2004 they organised a weekend conference for church members, and over 250 attended. Mary and I were no longer needed to initiate such events! We truly thanked God for the growth in spiritual life and responsibility that had taken place over these few years.

I had now been Field Director in Cambodia for 10 years. After this period of time, OMF's usual practice was to hand on the role to others, though we hoped to return after home assignment to do direct church-planting work ourselves. We felt at peace that we had completed what God had given us to do in this particular role of forming an OMF team in Cambodia. It would take new leadership to move OMF's work there to the next stage. From 10 members our team had grown to 85 adults and over 30 children from 17 different countries. God had gathered us together at an amazing rate. People had been attracted to join us because of our reputation for warm fellowship and care alongside the clear ministry goals that I felt God had given us. Unlike other OMF teams, most of our colleagues were still in their first few years of service, so our 20 years of ministry in Thailand provided valuable experience we could share with them. Certainly they lacked cultural and ministry experience, but they more than made up for it in their enthusiasm to serve the Lord.

During this time, the national church had continued to grow at an amazing 30% per year. From a membership of 18,000 in 200 churches in 1995, by 2005 it had grown to 260,000 members in 2,430 churches. As a team we were deeply privileged to have played a part in that. God had brought life from an ash heap, with his own people giving glory to him in this land.

On the evening of 28 February 2005 all the OMF Cambodia team members met for a historic meeting at the team centre. After a special meal we formally handed over the leadership of the OMF team to Dave and Fiona Rickards, followed by prayers of consecration. Gifts were exchanged, with many loving tributes and prayers.

It was now full-on packing of 10 years' accumulated stuff! Farewell church visits were fitted in, with many more prayers and much care expressed. After a lovely send-off from the team centre, we headed for the airport. We were leaving a precious country, now being transformed by the power of the gospel.

PART THREE

OPEN ROADS

THE UK

20

REDIRECTION

We arrived back in Manchester on a cold and windy day in March 2005. As we returned to warm welcomes at our sending churches in Manchester, Newcastle, and Glasgow, the remarkable growth of the Cambodian church grabbed people's attention. We were excited by the prospect of returning to Cambodia to do church planting in rural areas after our year in the UK. We reckoned we could do at least two more years' hands-on outreach work in Asia before returning to do further ministry in the UK.

As we began to consider this future work, we were constantly being confronted by how much had changed in our native country – not just since our last home assignment four years earlier, but also in the last 30 years of living in Asia! On a superficial level, there were changes like the new wheely bins for homes, speed cameras that had seemingly sprouted everywhere on the roads, or the fact door handles on trains had been replaced by buttons. All these changes made settling into daily life in the UK a challenge. What was much harder to catch up with was the change in values and expectations, both in society and in the church.

Looking ahead to our long-term future in the UK, we researched how many Cambodian and Thai people were now living in the country. We discovered that while there were only 1000 Cambodians living here, mostly south of London, there were 40,000–50,000 Thai people, scattered widely throughout the country. It seemed clear therefore that ministry among the Thai, when we eventually returned home, would be a strategic opportunity for us.

We had our plans. But as had happened before, the OMF leaders had a different idea for us to consider. The OMF UK North Region Director would be stepping down at the end of 2005 and no replacement was in view for at least a year. Would we take the role on an interim basis?

The proposal would most likely mean the end of our service in Asia. After the initial shock, we wondered if taking the role and staying in the UK might actually be God's will for us. It would allow us to deal with family responsibilities while continuing to be involved in world mission, supporting missionaries from the north region, and helping churches and individuals get involved in OMF's work.

My mother was becoming increasingly frail, and we now had primary responsibility for her care since my sister had moved to Canada. Mum was living in a retirement home over on the east coast in Grimsby, so fortnightly trips there were part of our regular programme now.

Though we were sad at not returning to Cambodia, we accepted the invitation and soon saw how God had overruled to keep us in the UK. We were ever conscious of God's oversight of our lives, assuring us that, 'I know the plans I have for you' (Jeremiah 29:11). In May 2006 we were able to help Mum celebrate her 90th birthday. She passed away two weeks later. We were thankful to be with her in her last days. We praised God too for her ongoing support for our overseas missionary service, despite the cost to herself as a widow for many years with few family members nearby.

We also discovered that that OMF had been praying for someone to initiate ministry among Thai people in the UK. They were excited to hear of our interest in this area and suggested we do that after my time as Regional Director finished.

We now realised that, if we were to work effectively among the Thai, we needed to be in the right place. Most of the Thai people living in the Manchester area lived in the south of the city, but our home was in the north, and was inaccessible by public transport. While we were enjoying living in the house provided by OMF for the North Regional Director, we looked for a suitable future home. It took five months to sell our house and another five months to get a new one. Finally, though, we had a place in the south that was easy to reach, and with rooms large enough for meetings. We gave thanks to God for his provision and perfect timing!

When the Regional Director role ended in February 2007, we gave our attention fully to serving Thai people in the UK. Before leaving the position, we had begun to connect with Thai people in the UK and learn more about their lives. On one occasion Mary and I went for lunch at a Thai restaurant in Altrincham, near Manchester. Seeing a picture of an attractive young lady on the wall, we asked the restaurant proprietor if this was her daughter. 'No,' she replied, 'it's a royal Thai princess!' Now we felt we were with friends, we chatted happily in Thai. A little later she asked us whether we would be willing to teach English to some of her staff who had difficulty communicating with customers.

Mary offered to teach the staff twice a week and agreed to be paid in Thai food! This continued for several years, and we became good friends with many of the restaurant staff. As several of them came to our home, we discovered more about what life was like for Thai people in the UK. For example, we learned that Christmas Day was the worst day of the year for them – everything was shut, and they had nowhere to go and nothing to do.

None of the Thai restaurant workers have yet come to a personal faith in Christ, but we still had opportunities to point them towards God, and remain in touch with them. As far as they were concerned, they were Thai and so were Buddhists, while we were British and Christians, our nationality dictating our religion. They had not yet met any Thai Christians, so for them a change of religion was out of the question. On a later occasion we were able to bring a Thai Christian to talk to them. The restaurant workers were astonished that it was possible to be both a Thai and a Christian. In the meantime, they were happy for us to pray with them about issues they faced in life. These experiences helped us see that the most fruitful way for us to serve in future would be to find and encourage existing Thai Christians to reach out to their fellow Thai in the UK.

In February 2006 God began to confirm the way ahead for us in ministry with Thai people in the UK. During a visit to one of our sending churches, International Harvest in Newcastle, we gave a brief update and shared about our anticipated ministry among the Thai. After they had prayed for us, the minister paused, before saying, 'As for this couple, God says, "The best is yet to come."' About ten minutes later, after we had sat down, another member of the congregation stood up and repeated exactly the same words.

These unexpected 'words of prophecy' given to us appeared to have been genuine. Not only were they an encouragement for us to press ahead in the Lord's service, but they have also been fulfilled in what the Lord has done through us among Thai people in the UK. Indeed, they mark one of the most fruitful periods of our ministry.

The foundation of this fruitfulness was prayer. In the middle of 2006 we had met up with Dennis and Jane Hardy, a couple who had served in Thailand as independent missionaries for several years and had recently returned to the UK. Together we shared our hopes that God would open a door of opportunity to minister to Thai people in the UK. We agreed to meet with them once a month to pray. This prayer time has continued for over 15 years, an expression of our ongoing dependence on the Lord. We send a personal monthly prayer letter to several hundred people, and also provide a weekly prayer bulletin. Such committed prayer support has been a foundation of our ministry.

For now, though, we were faced with the challenge of where to begin. Would there be any Thai Christians in the UK to help us reach out to other Thai people living here? We knew there were very few Christians in Thailand, around 0.2% of the population, and even fewer in the UK. We discovered that many of the Thai Christians who did live in the UK were not practising their faith. This was often due to their difficulties with British churches – not understanding the language used, struggling to feel part of the community, or not hearing preaching that seemed relevant to them. We also found some Thai Christian women were married to non-Christian British men who prevented them from going to church on Sundays.

It was a discouraging start. When we heard there were two Thai people attending a church in Liverpool, we headed over there to try and meet them, only to find they had temporarily returned to Thailand. Yet we continued praying each month with Dennis and Jane that the Lord would lead us to Thai Christians we could encourage. We also prayed that together we could reach out to other members of the Thai community who knew nothing of God's love.

The monthly prayer meetings carried on.

And on.

Then in August 2007, after a year of praying with Dennis and Jane along these lines, the first 'green shoots' began to appear.

21

GREEN SHOOTS

'There's a Thai Christian living in Harrogate,' a missionary colleague told us in early August 2007. Within days we were on the road and visiting Ms Mali.

We discovered she had already been in the UK for several years, having married a British man who later died. Befriended by a local Christian, she had accepted the invitation to attend a church. Warming to the friendship shown, she had been baptised. She didn't seem to fully understand why, but it was a start at least! A short while later we discovered another Thai believer in Harrogate, and eventually they met together with one or two other local Thai people to form a monthly fellowship group.

A few days after we met Ms Mali, a friend in Newcastle mentioned that he knew some Thai Christians. So we travelled up there to meet them, and were soon enjoying fellowship in Thai language. They had previously tried to start a meeting themselves, but without success. So they were delighted to accept our offer of helping to run a monthly Bible study in Thai.

A week later we heard a knock at our door in Manchester, and opened it to find a Thai couple standing there. She was a Christian; he was not. 'Can you make him a Christian?' she asked, 'as I want to marry him, but I can't until he believes!'

We promised we would do our best! We invited Notey and Bill to come for a meal a few days later and spent a valuable time talking through the gospel. Unusually for a Thai man, Bill had a Catholic background, which helped him understand the saving work of Christ. A few weeks later he accepted Jesus as his Saviour, and not long after that he and Notey were married!

We had spent almost a year in prayer. Now, in just one month, Thai believers and seekers were literally knocking at our door. We marvelled at our faithful God who hears and answers prayer!

September began with us enjoying a lovely meal in Bowness on the shores of Lake Windermere with an English–Thai couple, who had been referred to us by a missionary. The lady, Mrs Amporn, seemed keen to learn more, so we agreed to visit again.

That month passed in a flurry of activity. We travelled to Carlisle and met a Thai lady there; welcomed a young Thai believer into our home for a few days; and unexpectedly had a visit from a Christian Thai lady, her British husband, and their daughter, who all came to see us from Birmingham! We encouraged the lady to continue in the faith and hoped we could arrange something locally for her in the future.

The same month Peter and Prang, the Thai couple from Liverpool, appeared and stayed with us for three weeks while searching for a flat. When they eventually found one, they began hosting a weekly fellowship meeting, inviting Notey and Bill along with another Thai friend. Alongside Bible study and worship in Thai, snack food was a feature of these weekly meetings. On one occasion, when the Thai food was stacked up high, a latecomer enquired, 'What are you studying this evening?' 'Fasting' was the memorable reply!

In October we started a monthly fellowship group in South Shields and finished the month by inviting all our new Thai Christian friends – 10 believers and seekers – to our house for a day of fellowship. We sang worship songs, I preached, and we enjoyed delicious Thai food together. These days, and later weekends, of fellowship have been a regular fixture twice a year ever since.

News began to spread of these fellowship groups, where believers were encouraged and Thai friends heard the gospel in an informal setting – some of them coming to faith in Christ. Sensing that the Lord would continue to expand this ministry and to provide a structure that would enable the groups to grow, we asked Peter and Prang to give us a suitable name. They suggested Network of Thai Christians, widely known simply as NTC.

The goal of these local NTC groups was not to take members away from local churches and plant Thai churches. Rather, we wanted to build them up in faith so they could be more effective members of their local church. Our hope too was that they would become so spiritually bright and excited about their faith that they would share that with Thai friends and bring them to the Lord also. The warm fellowship in the groups would be an important factor in many non-Christian Thai coming to faith in Christ.

In just a few months we had already clocked up several thousand miles on the roads, an exciting start to serving Thai Christians in the UK. Spending quality time with the believers was vital for their spiritual growth, so regular visits to the groups became an essential pattern of our ministry to them.

In 2008 our ministry expanded in a surprising way. Expecting to be caring for a handful of Thai groups in the north of England, we were to discover the Lord's plans were much bigger than ours.

That summer our friend in Bowness, Mrs Amporn, was flying back to Thailand to visit her family and discovered that the Thai lady next to her on the plane was also a Christian. Mrs Nang was living in Worthing on the south coast of England and had been following Jesus for 17 years. In all that time, however, she had never met another Thai Christian. 'You should start a fellowship group – David and Mary will run it for you!' Amporn told her, since we had just started a group in Amporn's home.

Soon we found ourselves in Worthing, and before long a monthly group was meeting in Mrs Nang's home. One of her Buddhist friends liked what she heard so much that she threw her idols in the wheely bin and announced she was now a follower of Jesus. Other friends in the area were invited, and another thriving group was well underway.

Back in Bowness, Amporn's group was looking to grow and link up with Thai Christians in the larger town of Barrow. Mary remembered meeting a Thai Christian there while she was on home assignment 15 years earlier. We contacted churches in Barrow, asking if they knew of a Mrs Pongpan. No one had.

One day Amporn was out shopping in the area and, seeing a small group of Thai people, went over to chat to them. The conversation revealed one of them was called Pongpan. Amporn then asked her, 'Are you "the" Pongpan, a Christian?'

'That's me!' Pongpan replied.

Pongpan was excited to meet another Thai Christian, and when Amporn encouraged her to form a group in Barrow, she readily agreed. Pongpan had a hairdressing salon in Barrow, and many of her customers were Thai people. So before long she was inviting a steady stream of customers to come and sample Christian fellowship.

Those coming really enjoyed the warm friendship in the group. But when they began to realise the 'bite' of the gospel and the changes following Jesus would mean in their lives, they mostly stopped coming. Despite this discouragement, some persisted. One of them found solace in the gospel after being badly treated by her neighbours. Another lady attended regularly for a year before she announced, 'Last month I believed 80%. Today it is 100%!' Eventually she was baptised, and later led her mother, visiting from Thailand, to faith in Christ too.

Not all groups were so successful. Before long Peter and Prang's group in Manchester came to an end as they and the other members all graduated from their university courses and returned to Thailand. We were disappointed that these students were not with us long enough to be substantially built up in the faith. However, they were the start of a trickle of Thai people returning to Thailand who had come to or grown in their faith in the UK. Today a group of about 20 returnees to Thailand are in regular fellowship with each another. They continue to encourage one another in serving the Lord and his church there, an encouraging outflow of our work here in the UK.

We also realised that each fellowship group in the UK needed a long-term core membership to give stability and spiritual input to the students who joined them. A Manchester group restarted in 2010 when two Thai university lecturers accepted the Lord. They were subsequently joined by other long-term members, and the group has continued meeting ever since.

We now had five fellowship groups – enough to care for! But we still wondered if God had more in store for us.

22

DOORS OPEN WIDE!

Did Jacob expect to father 12 sons? From the account in Genesis 29–30 one wonders whether the experience of such a rapidly growing family took him somewhat by surprise! In the Thai work we likewise were both surprised and thrilled to see that, in the next 10 years, we had 12 groups that were active and growing. Each one had come into being in an unexpected way.

For example, our friend Ms Jah was still the only Thai believer in Carlisle. When she opened an Asian food store in October 2008, she invited us to come and commit it to the Lord. She also put some Thai gospel tracts near the entrance. When two Thai ladies wandered in, they saw the tracts and declared themselves to be Christians too. A new group in Carlisle had begun! That same day, a Thai man came into the shop and I was able to lead him to faith in Christ! Sadly, we never saw him again, but we trusted the Lord would continue to work in his life.

We now had groups in the north and south, and were praying for God to work in the Midlands. Then, in mid-2012, a breakthrough came. An unexpected phone call from an OMF colleague shared that he had located a Thai Christian in Huntingdon in Cambridgeshire. So at the first opportunity we crossed the country and met up with Mrs Pat, a keen Christian who had lived in Huntingdon for several years. Her son, Piak, was a Buddhist, but her daughter-in-law, Nam, was a Christian. Pat was happy to open her home for a monthly Thai meeting, and so Huntingdon now had a Thai group too. The group was blessed with earnest enquirers from the start, and eventually became one of our largest groups, numbering 15 members at times.

One unique event helped this growth. Nam was visiting her father in Thailand, seeking to lead him to faith in Christ before he died. While she was there talking to him, she got a phone call from Piak. 'I have just seen a vision of the Lord!' he said. 'Now I believe!'

This vision was repeated two days later, while Piak was driving home from work. Still in tears he parked the car, and immediately committed his life to Christ. Later, feeling called to serve the Lord full-time, Piak and Nam sold the Thai restaurant they were running and went to Bible college for three years. Today they are full-time members of OMF's team in the UK, seeking to reach Thai students for Christ.

Would there be more from the Midlands? At the autumn 2012 fellowship day in Manchester we welcomed a newcomer from Birmingham. Mrs Mem was very enthusiastic about starting a Thai group in her city, and within a month it was up and running. She took every opportunity to share the gospel with other Thai people in the factory where she worked and invited them to the meeting. She has since proved to be a caring 'under-shepherd' for the people in her group.

One of the first members of the Birmingham group was a middle-aged lady called Mrs Jum. She had a radiant faith, while at the same time carrying the burden of terminal cancer. Her caring spirit extended to both her grown-up daughters, who she often encouraged to trust in the Lord. Nearing the end of her life, she offered forgiveness to her husband, who had misbehaved with other women. Turning to Mary and me, she said, 'I will see you up there!' pointing heavenwards. Such faith was a real encouragement to us all.

Her funeral, perhaps the first for a Thai believer in the UK, was held in a large church in Birmingham, with many Thai visitors present. The Thai Christians sang a special worship song in Thai, a clear testimony to their enquiring friends.

As the number of groups began to grow, a sense of belonging together gradually began to develop. They had an identity as the Network of Thai Christians in UK, with its own national committee, website, and monthly prayer newsletter.

However, as the groups continued to grow, we felt that greater fellowship between groups would help build up the faith of the Thai believers. So the twice-yearly fellowship days became fellowship weekends, and then a summer camp was added.

In 2009 we took a step of faith and booked Blaithwaite House in the Lake District for our first four-day camp. Bible teaching was given by a Thai pastor brought over from Thailand, a full programme of teaching and games was organised, and lots of Thai food was provided. The camp became an annual event. As numbers grew steadily, we had to move to larger venues, and now welcome around 125 people a year.

We had reached our goal of 12 fellowship groups, but the growth has continued. As such we have experienced the truth that God 'is able to do immeasurably more than all we ask or imagine' (Ephesians 3:20).

At the time of writing, we have 15 groups in England and two in Scotland. In addition there are two fellowship weekends and an annual four-day camp. How could such a work be cared for and arranged, given the limited time and energy of Mary and me? We wondered what was the best way forward.

A great help has been the Thai committee of eight members, who are drawn from the different fellowship groups. They assist us in overseeing our plans and values as a para-church organisation. Registering the NTC organisation as a charity in 2020 has been another support, as it means that we now have a group of trustees to give overall guidance.

On the local level each of the fellowship groups has a leader and an assistant leader, and members take turns in leading worship, Bible study, and prayer, as well as providing hospitality. Sub-committees run the camp and other special activities.

As for Mary and me, we have intentionally reduced our travelling ministry to the groups, not least to encourage them to take increasing responsibility for their own growth and progress. We have realised that for the work to have a strong future, members of the network must have a full and active involvement.

Our vision is still to see more Thai fellowship groups established nationwide, so that every Thai believer and seeker can have access to a group who will establish and affirm their faith. Though now in my 80s, I hope – alongside Mary – to see the vision increasingly fulfilled in the coming days.

Looking back now on over 50 years of missionary service with the people of Southeast Asia, in three countries, how do I view it?

It has been a unique privilege to see God's hand working in many situations, bringing people who had never heard of Jesus before to faith in him, and seeing his church formed in different places. That divine hand has likewise been extended to us as God's servants, providing for us, protecting us, and using us for his kingdom work.

When I was called by God to world mission at the Keswick Convention in 1965, the Lord assured me that he would take responsibility for all that I needed – not only for my provision and welfare, but for wisdom and strength to be able to serve him effectively. That promise has been fulfilled throughout my ministry. When the call to mission was repeated in 1994, with the same promises, again the Lord has provided.

That call upon my life has been my 'inner motivating force'. It has kept me moving forward in serving the Lord, so that the many obstacles before me were there to be overcome rather than a reason to stop.

It is true that pain and fear and loss have been part of the journey, especially the loss of beloved colleagues and then my Jenny. But even there the Lord took me through the pain of separation.

Certainly along the way there have been mistakes, shortcomings, failures, and struggles. However, I trust that even in those God worked for good, as I looked to him.

Likewise when other colleagues have needed to retire from their missionary service, it has opened up a whole new ministry among the Thai who have come to stay in our country. That has been a special privilege.

Would I repeat the journey? By God's grace, yes. There is nothing greater in this world than being a servant of God, ready to follow his direction.

May we each give ourselves fully to such service, with a glad and thankful heart!

To God be the glory for all he has done!

EPILOGUE

A PRECIOUS RETURN

After Jenny and I left Tha Tako in 1985, the work there had never fully left my thoughts and prayers. It was so special therefore that on 1 April 2007, 22 years later, I was able to make a return visit there with Mary. Word had gone out that 'the teacher and his new wife' would be coming, and I was invited to preach at the morning service.

The Tha Tako church building, which Jenny and I had seen open the year we left, stood proudly to welcome us. It was now surrounded by an orchard of mature fruit trees, a beautiful picture of the church's growth in maturity since I had left. A good number of the church members had gathered from both Tha Tako and Pai Sali, and Mary and I were welcomed like the 'return of the patriarchs' with great love and affection. We were moved to see that most of the early believers were continuing steadfastly with the Lord, now joined by others new to the faith.

Mrs Roy from Pai Sali was there to welcome us, though we learned that her sister, Mrs Jarey, and Mr Yuang (our first host there) had both gone to be with the Lord. Among those welcoming us from Tha Tako were Mr Snguan, still the main church leader, and Mr Gram, the former assassin and builder who oversaw the construction of the Tha Tako church. Wonderfully, several of the members' children were now taking leadership roles in the church.

Though Miss Lawt was not there with us, we heard that she and her husband, Chai, were not only going well with the Lord but were now the leaders of the growing church in Tak Fa.

After I had preached and encouraged everyone to continue steadfastly in the Lord, many of them shared stories of how the Lord had been with them and blessed them in their daily lives. What was striking in most of their testimonies was that they quoted Bible verses we had taught them from the earliest days.

We reluctantly left them, but rejoiced at how our hopes of establishing a Christian community in the area, where previously there had been none, had been fulfilled beyond our expectations. This work was not ours alone, but also that of many other missionaries and local Christian colleagues, especially the Fietje family, who paid a heavy price with Koos' untimely death. As we departed, we were mindful of the promise 'you know that your labour in the Lord is not in vain' (1 Corinthians 15:58). What a deep privilege to have helped this group of people come to know and love the Lord, and to pass the gospel on to those yet to hear it.

We hope you've enjoyed David's story of God's faithfulness.

David Robinson serves with OMF International, which was founded by James Hudson Taylor in 1865 as the China Inland Mission.

We serve the Church and share the good news of Jesus Christ in all its fullness with countries across East Asia. We're for all Christians who want to be relevant in mission. We're a forward-thinking gospel-focused movement that pursues every avenue to reach East Asians for Jesus. In a changing world, we need to find the most effective means possible.

Today this looks like around 1,400 workers from 40 countries serving across East Asia. Their ministries vary from church planting to medical work, from sport to theological education. Each of them seeks to serve the Church and share the good news of Jesus Christ in all its fullness.